ORDERING THE EVIDENCE:
VOLVERÁS A REGIÓN
AND
CIVIL WAR FICTION

BIBLIOTECA UNIVERSITARIA PUVILL

DIRIGEN

Josep Puvill Valero. Puvil Libros S.A.
Josep M. Solà-Solé. The Catholic University of America

II. ENSAYOS. 9

MALCOLM ALAN COMPITELLO

ORDERING THE EVIDENCE:
VOLVERÁS A REGIÓN
AND
CIVIL WAR FICTION

PUVILL LIBROS S.A.

Barcelona

© Malcolm Alan Compitello
Publicado por Puvill-Editor, 1983

DISTRIBUIDOR
PUVILL LIBROS S.A.
Boters, 10 - Paja, 29
y Jaime I,5
Barcelona-2

Publicado con la ayuda de Intercambios Culturales
Hispano-Americanos

Dep. Legal: Z-1968-83
I.S.B.N.: 84-85202-38-4
IMPRESO EN ESPAÑA

Talleres gráficos: INO-Reproducciones S.A.
                    Santa Cruz de Tenerife, 3
                    Zaragoza-7

DEDICATION

For the women in my life: Patricia, Gina, Rose and Pamela, and to the memory of my father Pasquale J. Compitello "en el buen sentido de la palabra bueno."

CONTENTS

CONTENTS

PREFACE

Few events have so decisively effected a country's historical and cultural development, nor so polarized world opinion and the arts as did the Spanish Civil War of 1936-1939. The destruction, loss of life, and psychological maiming ensuing from the conflict were enormous. But in many ways those losses pale before the deleterious consequences the war's outcome was to portend for Spaniards. The Nationalist victory installed as government a regime forged during the war itself. Its leader wielded power until his demise almost forty years later. Policies undertaken by the oligarchical forces controlling that political system purposefully let the wounds opened by the war fester rather than make any attempt to suture them.

It is not surprising, then, that the war's effects were still perceptible to a young doctoral student making his first trip to Spain in 1971. Imbued with a fascination for modern Spanish literature nurtured by reading and research about the literature of Spain's most recent outbreak of fratricidal hostilities, he became acutely aware of manifestations of francoism's repressive presence in the workplace. Guardia Civil and the ever-present Policía Armada ringed the new campus of Madrid's Universidad Autónoma, constantly on the lookout for any excuse that would allow them to exercise the repressive presence already too evident at the Compultense. Colleagues complained of the restrictive policy decisions handed down by the Ministerio de Educación y Ciencia. Materials to be multicopied had to be scrutinized and faculty meetings approved by the dean's office. These were only a few barometers of the less than adequate freedom granted the university community.

11

Receiving the Losada edition of Antonio Machado's *Obras completas* in a plain brown wrapper at the Insula bookstore, and coming to the awareness that material on Spain's recent past was more accessible in the comfortable library left behind than in the country with which it dealt made one focus on the struggle for access to knowledge characteristic of Spanish intellectual life.

While the eyes saw everywhere the civil conflict's lasting effects, the ears heard the francoist regime severely criticized in private conversations and in the secure public forum offered by the Instituto Internacional on Calle Miguel Angel. Yet those same eyes began to read accounts of how Spain was forging a new present that was enabling it to place its bloody war in the deepest recesses of collective cultural memory. Other reading followed which attempted to demonstrate how cultural production was moving beyond the ideological divisions of previous periods and into one characterized by more "universal" thematic concerns and complex artistic structures —the product, in great part, of artists who now disavowed the efficacity of committed stances sustained only a few years before. Subsequent study of Civil War narrative, francoism's nature, and the trajectory described by post-Civil War fiction's evolution followed in an attempt to reconcile the paradoxical perceptions just noted. Out of that search the present study began to take shape.

As time passed it became apparent that solving this specific problem of literary criticism hinged on the resolution of an even more fundamental one: the relationship between social structure and artistic creation. Subsequent reading in modern poetics underscored both the lack of any coherent methodological grounding in previous studies treating Civil War fiction, and the inability to reconcile this aspect of relating artifact and social group until the matter of method was addressed.

This monograph represents the results of meditation on these complex issues. If offers a reassessment of Civil War fiction characterized by a fundamental methodological displacement that distances it from previous literature in the field. A methodological reordering of the type undertaken here allows for a more efficient calibration of social structure's impact on literature, a topic whose referentiality extends beyond the particular circumstances studied herein. It also rectifies some misconceptions about the nature of the particular society (Franco's Spain) expressed in earlier critical works.

To test the hypotheses underlying the methodology, I chose to analyze what many critics believe to be the most complex narrative treatment of the Spanish Civil War produced under francoism: *Volverás a Región*, written by the enigmatic Juan Benet Goitia. The decision to concentrate on one text instead of offering anthological treatment of many was made for several reasons. It was thought that thorough treatment of one specific narrative whose surface seemingly belies the critical assumptions upon which this monograph is based would underscore the method's effectiveness in dealing with even the most difficult of narratives and, thus, provide a complete exercising of its capacities. Moreover, this choice would allow for the presentation of a differing opinion of the work and author that became, along with the initial problem I set out to solve, the other component of a scholarly passion that has encompassed much of my investigation to date.

Many people deserve my thanks for the help provided in a number of ways. Miguel Enguídanos transmitted to me his passionate interest in the Civil War and its literature. John Dyson demonstrated time and time again during the apprenticeship I served as Assistant Editor of *The American Hispanist*, that form of argumentation is as important as concept. Merle Simmons, Russell Salmon, and Joseph Ricapito deserve my eternal gratitude for standing by a young scholar and refusing to let a career end before it started. Walter Mignolo and especially Juan Ignacio Ferreras taught by example the importance of a method.

To my colleagues at Michigan State University, Freida Brown, Robert Fiore, Michael Koppisch, and William Blake Tyrrell, and to David Herzberger of the University of Connecticut go my thanks for having read and/or discussed with me so constructively various aspects of this project.

13

My deepest appreciation goes to Patricia Brooks, who read the entire manuscript numerous times in the course of its elaboration and who, most of all, always had faith, and surrendered so much to enable this work to be completed.

Portions of Chapters I and III appeared in *The American Hispanist* as "*Volverás a Región*, The Critics, and The Civil War." Support offered by the All-University Research Grants provided by Michigan State University aided in both the research and production of this monograph, as did a generous grant from the Spanish-American Cultural Exhange, INC (HISPAM). I thank its President, Dr. Josep María Sola-Solé and the administration at Michigan State University for their assistance.

As final proofs for this book were being read, Juan Benet published Herrumbrosas lanzas Libros I-VI *(Madrid: Alfaguara, 1983). This novel, the first of a multi-work series dealing with the civil war, is once again set in Región. Its publication reconfirms Benet's interest in this historical event. It remains to be seen if it will have the impact on Spanish fiction that* Volverás a Región *has had. Benet's latest work deals with many of the characters and situations found in* Volverás a Región. *While a reading of the latter in the light of subsequent reelaborations of actors and situations enriches the complex intertextual web Benet has built up around Región, it in no way alters the argumentation presented by this monograph, for the autonomy of each of the author's texts as an object of study must be respected.*

I also learned that Vicente Cabrera's book on Benet for the Twayne World Author Series has appeared (Boston: G.K. Hall, 1983). While I have not had the opportunity to examine it, I assume that the unpublished article by Cabrera quoted in my book has been incorporated into his Twayne volume.

CHAPTER I

The Novel, The Critics, and The Spanish Civil War: A socio-Poetic Reappraisal

Introducion

It is current practice in many quarters to view literary criticism and theory as mutually exclusive. I do not share that belief, but rather see them as activities existing at different levels of analytical conception. It is hoped that this study will demonstrate that it is possible to intersect both planes and serve, simultaneously, critical and theoretical ends. Within the parameters of contemporary Spanish fiction my remarks provide a reevaluation of the body of criticism generated by fiction dealing with the Spanish Civil War. An alternative model for dealing with such narrative exists, one which is valid for all prose fiction produced during the francoist period of Spanish history.[1] That the model's validity can be exended to any fictional discourse, especially that produced under repressive regimes, is an undeveloped but fully integrated element of the theory.

At the level of meta-theoretical discourse the pages that follow attempt a reflection on the complex relationships between historical epoch, world view/ideology, and their expression in narrative form. The basis for both my discrepancies with previous critical assessments

---

1. For the sake of convenience I define the francoist period as the time span from the end of the Spanish Civil War in April, 1939, to Franco's death in November, 1975. I have adopted this expedient so as to concentrate on the post-war era since prose fiction of this period is the main focus of this study. However, the francoist period can best be described as the era in which Francisco Franco exercised almost complete control over Spanish government. This period begins with his installation as head of state during the war and with his death. Franco's presence in Spanish power structures did, in fact, continue after his death as can be attested by the policies of the monarchy's first government headed by Carlos Arias Navarro, who, several years earlier, had been Franco's hand-picked choice to succeed Carrero Blanco as president of the government after the latter's assassination.

17

of Civil War fiction, and for the new model I propose is decidedly sociological. As such, the method is rooted in the dialectical sociology of Lucien Goldmann and his followers. However, I have modified Goldmann's method so as to have the means for a more coherently elaborated analysis of the relationship between narrative structure, especially at the syntactical level, and the manifestation therein of a given world view. In this way it is hoped that an analytical tool will be established that will work through the immanence of the text to societal mediation.

Critics and Civil War Fiction: A Review

Almost every study on the post-war Spanish novel addresses itself to narrative presentations of the Spanish Civil War. Nevertheless, the amount of Spanish fiction dealing with the war far outstrips the critical attention such works have received, despite the expanding rate at which criticism on the subject is being published. Several reasons may explain this paradoxical situation. Inside Spain the rigid censorial system of the francoist period dampened the desire of many who might have wished to discuss polemical aspects of this literature. In addition, to Hispanic scholars working both inside Spain and elsewhere, literature treating the war was seen as less interesting than other types of fiction, particularly in recent years, as Spanish narrative became more elaborate and structurally complex.

Although not numerous, studies on the topic are interesting, and should be considered in any reevaluation of the matter[2]. While both the methodologies and conclusions of these investigations are diverse, certain constant elements are fequently shared. In terms of methodology, many of the approaches to the subject are classificatory rather than analytical. Few have bridged the gap between literary history and

---

2. The bibliographic data upon which my conclusions are based can be found in my recent article "The Novel, the Critics, and the Civil War: A Bibliographic Essay," *Anales de la Narrativa Española Contemporánea*, 4 (1979), 117-138.

criticism. This is due in part to a methodological constant: the critics' concentration on extracting the authors' ideas from the works' content, a tendency directly related to the nature of this literature. As 5 many of the novels studied are fictional reconstructions of historical events, or use them as backdrops, it is easy to view such works as historical "documents" from which the analyst is free to extract the author's opinions. Such approaches are, finally, self-defeating, in my view, for they deny the work its primordial existence as fictional discourse. Writers have open to them many rhetorical and organizational avenues through which they may express their ideas, and in much modern fiction structure bears meaning just as content does.

Most of the criticism also arrives at similar conclusions about fiction and the Civil War. The passage of time has seen a diminution of the violently partisan ideological diatribes that characterized narrative produced during the hostilities and in the first years of the francoist era. The events of the war, and its motivation, became hazier in the minds of Spaniards, who were more concerned with their day-to-day existence in francoist Spain. Consequently, the war became less important. Therefore, as generations grew up that had not experienced the period of belligerency directly (either as participants, or as children suffering it during their formative years), they have gradually forgotten the war and its effects. Writers now take a more ecumenical view when treating the topic. Rather than being supportive of one ideological view or the other, they look "beyond ideology" to the causes of the war, condemn the evil in both sides, and express a deep sense of regret for the Spanish tragedy, which many view as having been inevitable, one more instance of the long history of Spaniard killing Spaniard.

There is also a direct link posited between this ideological relaxation and the marked improvement perceptible in the quality of war fiction. As novelists become less concerned with supporting one group or the other, their works become better pieces of literature, capable of standing on their own intrinsic merits. This type of postulation characterizes not only appraisals of narrative concerning the Civil War, but those dealing with fiction of the francoist era in general. Supposedly, peninsular fiction begins to work out the disastrous effects that the War and its outcome held for all cultural activity in Spain. As the country changed, so did the novel, and narrative fiction began to regain some of its past glory.

Such perceptions can in part be attributed to the desire of authors and critics alike to emphasize the improvement in the quality of Spanish literature in the past few years, even at the expense of the archievments of antecedent literary modes,[3] that have been ridiculed or forgotten. These changes, sometimes amounting to complete reversals of previously held views, are carried over into the realm of criticism, which for almost a decade has heralded the birth of a "new" Spanish literature, one that now charts a path parallel to the one followed by Spanish-American fiction. Critics are quick to point out that like the latter, Spanish fiction is now oriented toward more universal and existential problems, and has left behind its somewhat provincial preoccupation with strictly Spanish concerns.

Toward a Socio-Poetic Model

A substantial gap exists between my view of the topic under discussion in this chapter and the conclusions summarized above. This divergence is due partly to methodological differences. Central to my dissent, however, is the manner in which these studies perceive the relationship between ideology and literature on the one hand, and the evaluation of Spanish society under Franco on the other.

A non-partisan exposition of a problem in a literary work does not increase that text's intrinsic value as art. What is more, reasons exist to place in doubt commonly held assertions that Spanish literature aban-

3.   The most striking example of this is the disrepute into which socially oriented narrative fell during the late 1960's and early 1970's. This formerly dominant strain in serious peninsular fiction, and the theoretical texts that supported it lost their appeal. Many authors now reject its theories and accomplishments out of hand, saying that literature should confine itself to being good literature and not be concerned with trying to change the country's socio-political environment.

20

doned specifically national problems in an attempt to seek some illusive concept called "universality". Spanish fiction changes its manner of criticizing the francoist regime, not its manifestation of disaffection with the socio-political situation.

No one will deny that Spanish narrative underwent a tremendous stylistic and structural renovation triggered, in part, by the appearance of Luis Martin-Santos' *Tiempo de silencio* in 1962, which questioned some of the fundamental premises regulating serious Spanish narrative during the previous decade. While this change led to the production of a more sophisticated type of narrative fiction, it did not signal an abrogation of socially critical intent. From a straight-forward denunciation of ills through the work's content, more recent fiction has moved to a subtler type of denunciation. Such a change implies a redirection of readership as well. No longer bent on attempting to change Spanish society through the medium of his novel, the writer now directed his message at an intellectual elite with the requisite literary competence to understand complexly structured narrative messages. This indirect manner of criticism may be viewed by some as an abandonment of social goals, or as an attempt to achieve more universal appeal. Yet much of the best Spanish narrative is still, in my opinion, inexorably linked to the socio-political climate in Spain. Its main point of reference is, either directly or indirectly, the specificity of its own socio-political environment. To highlight the universal at the expense of the latter seems to me a misrepresentation of the meaning underlying the content and structure of the text.

Such an assertion is supported by serious studies of Spain's socioeconomic and cultural organization during the francoist period.[4] These works belie assessments of literary critics who believe that fundamental changes in the nature of Spain which occurred in the 1960's produced a literature that became less ideologically mediated by its

4. Relevant documentation and an in-depth discussion of this topic can be found in my doctoral dissertation "Ordering the Evidence: The Vision of the Spanish Civil War in Post-War Spanish Fiction, Indiana Univesity, 1979 and my unpublished essay "The Cultural Ideologies of Franco's Spain."

environment. In my estimation the repressive nature of the francoist regime and its desire to subsume artistic expression to its needs caused a division in the country's cultural sector based on a broad ideological cleavage. On the one hand were those who, through their creative works, either openly or tacitly supported the regime; on the other were intellectuals who voiced some type of opposition to it. It is from this dichotomy that I derive the two broad ideological groupings which, for the purpose of this study, will be termed pro-and anti-regime. It is this ideological stance with respect to the environment in which he works that underlies the artist's endeavors. Disagreement with the nature of the regime and its policies will be actualized in a literature that in some way is critical of them. It also engenders a rejection of the works belonging to the opposite ideological group. The situation with regard to the supporters of the regime is obviously just the opposite.[5]

The pro-regime ideology is a direct carry-over into the post-war period of the francoist principles forged during the war. It was a short step from portraying it as a crusade, and Franco as the reincarnation of the Cid or Pelayo, to post-war campaigns heralding a new Spanish empire, or the intellectual elaboration of a theory to explain and justify the role of *El Caudillo*. This imperial design is evident in such works as Rosales' and Vivanco's massive anthology/ "study" *Poesía heróica del imperio*. It finds its quintessential expression in the officially inspired

5. I would consider tacitly supportive of the regime such projects as the so-called *novela católica* that received a degree of critical attention in the 1950's. The *novela metafísica* proposed in the following decade by Manuel García Viñó falls into the same category.

  The *novela católica* manifested no apparent signs of belligerent triumphalism. In my opinion, however, a Catholic novel that did not protest the immoral actions of the regime and the manner in which the Spanish clergy participated in them, results in tacit support of the status quo.

  The *novela metafísica* was determined to free Spanish narrative from its pre-ocupation with specifically Spanish topics. To do this it vehemently criticized the social novel of this period. By advocating the treatment of non-Spanish themes, and by attacking one of the literary modes that was most vocal in its opposition to the regime, it was effectively allowing itself to be co-opted by francoism's ideological goal for the cultural sector: the abandonment of realistic assessments of the Spanish situation, and attacks on those who opposed it.

22

"epic" literature of the period and, most especially in Franco's own novel/film script *Raza*,[6] penned under the pseudonym Jaime de Andrade.

In additon to propagating a false image of Spain, reclothed as a new empire, such pro-regime representations contain two other important elements: an attack on those who supported the Loyalist cause during the war, or who opposed official positions after it, and the evasion of a direct portrayal of Spain's socio-economic reality. The former was linked to the regime's decision not to seek a reconciliation with its opponents once the war ended. This attitude of intransigence substantially contributed to the institutionalization of the cleavage betwen winners and losers. The long exile of many of Spain's pre-war intellectuals is directly attributable to it. The cultural manifestation of this attitude can be found in both criticism and creative literature written during and after the war. In its most patent cases, pro-francoist heros are presented as exemplary of all human virtues, while their opponents are iconographically depicted as sub-human anti-Spanish ogres.

Attempts to evade the presentation of reality are obviously tied to the presentation of a false imperial image, since both are distortions of the truth. The second tendency helps to explain the flood of translations of second-rate foreign works available on the market, as they had nothing to do with the Spanish ambience. The stage best demonstrated this officially inspired evasion. As José Monleón has described in

6. Román Gubern's *Raza. Un ensueño del general Franco* (Madrid: Ediciones 99, 1977) provides an interesting analysis of this work. An article written during the war by Benito Perojo, "Hacia la creación de una cinematografía nacional," *Vertice: Revista Nacional de la Falange*, No. 1 (April 1937), points out the triumphalist role reserved for cinema in the francoist regime.

He ahí la labor suprema de la cinematografía nacional: infundir en la conciencia colectiva la nobleza de tal misión; contribuir a dar a la paz un sentido laborioso, justiciero, fraternal y patriótico. Crear, en fin, un ideal: el ideal del trabajo con fines nacionales. Llevemos esta obra a los hogares españoles y la paz estará hinchada de cordialidad. Llevemos esta obra al extranjero, y daremos al mundo la impresión expléndida de que la España con que sueña el general Franco, y a que todos aspiramos, ha realizado sus ideales. Una España orientada sobre esas bases, será siempre Grande, Unida, Libre (no page).

Treinta años de teatro de derecha (Barcelona: Tusquets, 1971), theater offering a realistic presentation of Spain was totally absent from the Spanish stage for years, having been replaced with an endless succession of bedroom comedies and revivals of works by second-rate playwrights.

An explanation of the anti-regime ideology is not as simple. Nevertheless, certain structural constants are perceptible in such thought, even if the content of this group's component elements vary. In specific terms this ideology is prone to see the war in terms of the effects that its outcome held out for Spain. The institutionalization of the francoist regime perpetuated a system that effectively strangled the country, and that provided only surface prosperity and semi-freedom. In essence it served to fix post-war Spain's fate in such a way as to lead it on a one-way down-hill path to decadence and disintegration, a path that was clearly perceptible only during the later years of the francoist regime, and after its demise. Its origins come in part from the Loyalist ideological opposition to the Nationalists during the Civil War. The basis for this ideological viewpoint is essentially tied to disenchantment with or outright hostility to the socio-political, economic and cultural space that was now Spain. This reaction comes from both those who participated in the war, and had remained in the country, and the second generation of writers who suffered the effects of the period of belligerency during their childhood or adolescence. Intellectual opposition to the regime does not remain confined to those who had voiced their opposition to it from the start. It incorporated over the years dissidents from within the pro-regime ideological camp, and obviously the voices of younger generations as well. This assertion is supported by the following schematization of the Spanish intellectual sector (1936-1974) taken from Bejamín Ultra's *Pensar en Madrid* (Barcelona: Euros, 1976).

Oltra's data also supports my assertion that Spain's intellectuals can be grouped into two polar camps that in part originate in the Republican/Nationalist division of the Civil War. Those elements of the francoist camp that split with it and were incorporated into the

24

main trunk of the opposition are the liberal Falangists and Christian Democrats. Among them are men who played an important role in the regime's creation, institutionalization and administration such as Ridruejo, Aranguren, Laín Entralgo, and Ruiz Giménez. While this polar dichotomy does not remain homogeneous through the decades of francoist rule, the basic schism persists. To negate the existence of such an ideological cleavage is to handicap oneself in an approach to Spanish narrative and, by extension, all cultural production of the francoist era.

The failure of much literary criticism to analyze, or, in some cases, even to admit this cleavage has severely limited its ability to assess successfully fiction written in this period. Another fundamental methodological problem also obfuscated accurate analysis of narrative fiction written during this epoch. Many critics went only to the work's content where they believed that the author's ideas or ideology were directly manifested. Such an approach necessarily obscures the work's intrinsic existence as literature and not as social document.

Such fundamental problems as these led me to root my own theoretical construct in a method that I believe deals effectively with them: the dialectical literary sociology of Lucien Goldmann and his followers, principally as seen in the work of the noted Hispanic scholar Juan Ignacio Ferreras.[7]

At the center of Goldmann's method is the perception of the link between individual creation and societal mediation. Goldmann postulated that underlying the aesthetic organization of any given cultural text was the manifestation of a world view (what I label ideology) of the collective subject (societal grouping) into which the individual author and his thought can be inscribed.[8] His understanding of this cen-

---

7. Ferreras' well-known and numerous studies on modern Hispanic literature make him the most important dialectical literary sociologist in the field of Spanish studies. Particularly noteworthy is his recent *Fundamentos de sociología literaria* (Madrid: Cátedra, 1980). He has also contributed a fundamental analysis of Goldmann's method: "La sociología de Lucien Goldmann," *Revista de Occidente*, NS 105 (December 1971), pp. 311-336.

8. While Goldmann is insistent upon the fact that a world view is almost always asso-

tral concept is defined in his fundamental study *The Hidden God*. "What I have called a 'world vision' is a convenient term for the whole complex of ideas, aspirations and feeling, which links together members of a social group (a group which in most cases assumes the existence of a social class) and which opposes it to members of other social groups."[9]

While his critics have attacked the concept of collective consciousness as a diminution of the role of the individual artist in literature, nothing could be further from the truth. This idea implies no more than the assertion that an author's participation in a group inserted in a given socio-economic orden mediates his cultural production. Furchermore, Goldmann, more than most of those who criticize him, stresses the importance of the individual and his work, since it is here, in a specific cultural creation, that the collective subject's world view finds its most coherent expression.

Homology is the other fundamental component of Goldmann's method. He replaces the notion of analogy between the content of a given work of art and that of a group's thought with the idea that a parallel exists between aesthetic organization or structure of a text and the structure of the thought of the author's collective subject. As Goldmann states in one of his most important theoretical pronouncements:

> On this point, genetic structuralism has represented a total change of orientation—its basic hypothesis being precisely that the collective character of literary creation derives from the fact that the *structures* of the world of the work are homologous with the mental structures of certain social groups or is in intelligible relation with them, whereas on the level of content, that is to say, of the creation of imaginary worlds governed by these structures, the writer has

ciated with a social class, Ferreras utilizes a wider definition of groups possessing world views. He argues this point convincingly in "Le problème du sujet collectif en littérature," *Actes, Picaresque Espagnole. Etudes Sociocritiques* (Montpellier: CERS, 1976), pp. 56-67.

9. Lucien Goldmann. *The Hidden God*, trans. Phillip Thody (London: Routledge and Kegan Paul, 1970), p. 17.

total freedom. The use of the immediate aspect of his individual experience in order to create these imaginary worlds is no doubt frequent and possible but in no way essential, and its elucidation constitutes only a useful secondary task of literary analysis.[10]

In short, works with widely varying contents can express the same world view.[11]

Taken in tandem, homology and world view point directly to the need for a fundamental revision of how critics have approached the employment of the Civil War in post-war narrative, and, by extension, the analysis of the society/author/fictive act relationship in francoist Spain. World view is linked to the collective subject's own socio-political circumstances. Novels dealing with the Civil War written by authors whose world view is mediated by francoism would thus present a vision whose artistic structure is homologous to the structure of the group's reaction to that mediating agent, ones I have classified as either pro- or anti-regime. In other words, while the content of such narrative discourses treat the war, the novel expresses, at the level of structural organization, a response to the environment in which it was engendered. The Civil War, then, is not as important to the comprehension of the work's meaning as it is to an awareness of what the way it is represented implies for the world vision of the collective subject. The difference between such an approach and the type used by critics who previously assessed the topic is evident. The majority of them perceived the text as socio-historical document, and equated the image of the war presented in the text's content with the author's view of it. This is, of course, a perfect example of the type of reflective content analysis that the dialectical model transcends. A similar problem

10. "The Genetic-Structuralist Method in the History of Literature," in *Towards a Sociology of the Novel*, trans. Alan Sheridan (Cambridge: Tavistock Publications, 1975), p. 159.

11. As Goldmann points out in *Marxisme et sciences humaines* (Paris: Gallimard, 1970) "des contenus entièrement hétérogènes et meme opposés sont structurellement homologues ou bien se trouvent dans un rapport fonctionel sur le plan des structures catégoriques" (p. 58).

plagues the study of the post-war novel in general. Critics have looked for an analogy between a given work's narrative content and the author's commitment vis-à-vis Spain's socio-political environment during the francoist years. Typical of such criticism would be those studies whose classificatory system judges as social novels only those whose content deals with problems concretely verifiable in Spain's social structure.

The hypotheses of the Goldmannian model have many advantages for the critic. On the one hand they point out the necessity for inserting literature, or any cultural creation, into the overall structure of a given society. At the same time, reservations from some critical sectors to the contrary, it insists on the primacy of the literary work. Since its analysis is undertaken at the level of aesthetic organization, it does not allow the work to be "culled" as a mere social document. It also exonerates much modern and structurally complex fiction from the harsh criticism of more traditional or "orthodox" Luckacsian Marxist criticism which asserts that such "modernist" texts' abandon-

Goldmann's methodology consists of two interrelated levels of analysis, which he describes in *The Hidden God:* "The dialectical historian sets out from the significant structure of the facts which he intends to study, and aims to fit this structure into another and more comprehensive one that will provide an historical framework for it" (p. 102). Comprehension, the first level of analysis, is immanent in the work. It consists of the "...description, aussi précise que possible, d'une structure significative."[12] It is an attempt to describe, as fully as possible, the aesthetic structures of the work of art in which the homology with the mental structures of the collective subject's world is to be found. Explanation, the second step in this type of analysis, goes beyond the immanence of the text. "Le second plan, celui de l'explication, doit aboutir à une mise en relation fonctionnelle du modèle structurel, qui constitue l'unité de la signification de l'oeuvre, et des aspirations d'un sujet—relation qui permette d'insérer l'oeuvre en tant

12. *Ibid.,* p. 65.

qu'élément significatif et fonctionnel dans un totalité plus vaste.[13] These two levels of analysis are two phases of the same dialectical approach rather than two distinct processes. Goldmann illustrates this fact with an example from his own work:

> This method has, among others, the double advantage first of conceiving the whole set of human facts in a unitary manner and, then, of being both *comprehensive* and *explanatory*, for the elucidation of a significatory structure constitutes a process of *comprehension*, whereas its insertion into a larger structure is, in relation to it, a process of *explanation*. Let us take an example: to elucidate the tragic structure of Pascal's *Pensées* and Racine's tragedies is a process of comprehension; to insert them into extremist Jansenism by uncovering the structure of this school of thought is a process of comprehension in relation to the latter, but a process of explanation in relation to the writings of Pascal and Racine; to insert extremist Jansenism into overall history of Jansenism is to explain the first and to understand the second. To insert Jansenism, as a movement of ideological expression, into the history of seventeenth-century *noblesse de robe* is to explain Jansenism and to understand the *noblesse de robe*. To insert the history of the *noblesse de robe* into the over-all history of French society is to explain it by understanding the latter, and so on. Explanation and understanding are not therefore two different intellectual processes, but one and the same process applied to two frames of reference.[14]

The starting point for such an analysis is thus the text itself. Nevertheless, while Goldmann's assertion that the only valid starting point for sociological analysis is the empirically verifiable facts, the investigator does bring to his analysis a working hypothesis formulated

13. Lucien Goldmann, "Littérature (Sociologie de la), "in *Enciclopaedia Universalis* (Paris: Enciclopaedia Universalis France, S.A., 1968), p. 8.

14. Goldmann, "The Genetic-Structuralist Method," pp. 162-163.

from his knowledge of a given area. Ferreras admits as much in his important *Revista de Occidente* article.

> Creo también, aunque es tema delicado, que lo que propugna Goldmann se parece más a la inducción que a la deducción, aunque ambos métodos se encuentran siempre inexplicablemente unidos. Inducir sobre el objeto a partir de las deducciones de una hipótesis, sería quizá la formulación más correcta para esta sociología (p. 329).

My insistence on this clarification is necessary since the methodology developed in this study conforms to the way Ferreras assesses the relationship between induction and deduction in Goldmann. For this and other reasons, adjustments have been made in my adaptation of Goldmann's method.

To begin with, certain aspects of the explanative level must be presented as prior hypothesized conditions for performing the analytical operations at the comprehensive level. Part of this has already been delineated in the portions of this study where I established the two antagonistic world views and corresponding collective subjects perceptible in francoist Spain. Such a description is viewed as a necessary first step because of the way previous studies have either ignored or misconstrued this material. At the same time, the elaboration and explanation of the world view of the author (Juan Benet) with whose important novel (*Volverás a Región*) I will test my model must precede the analysis of the text particularly because most criticism of this text is of the type I described above. That is to say, it perceives no ideological intent underlying Benet's presentation of the Civil War. Furthermore, Benet's newness as an object of critical study warrants such a treatment, if only to clear up some of the misconceptions that surround various aspects of his work and personality, most especially his expressed views of francoist Spain, the ambience in which *Volverás a Región* was produced.

The second modification introduced involves the study of narrative syntax. Operations at each successive level (as described in detail in the pages that follow) are analyzed at the comprehensive level and then immediately inserted into the larger context at the explanative one before proceeding to the subsequent syntagmatic element. This has been done so as to maintain a symmetry and continuity to the study of *histoire* and *discours*.

While his theory's capacity to isolate and rectify existing critical misperceptions is acknowledged, Goldmann's methodology leads to problems of application when the analyst turns to a specific text. Its ability to elucidate the work's structural organization is incomplete, and Goldmann's own interpretive essays are too intuitive to be of use as guides. What is more, they exclude the advances that modern poetics has made in studying the literary language of a given discourse, advances that have markedly enriched the appreciation of meaning in fiction. Thus, while I am in agreement with Goldmann's criticism of modern poetics' a-historical hypotheses, as analytical tools, these new modes are of fundamental importance and aid to the researcher. As with Goldmann's own, they emphasize the primacy of the literary artiefact by demonstrating the meaning-bearing aspects of the structural disposition of such fiction.

The combination of such disparate entities would appear to be unfruitful. Such a co-joining, however, benefits both elements. Too often structuralist approaches remain at the descriptive level, leaving meaning or ideology out of their discussions. If this factor is discussed it is normally at a level of abstraction that removes it from an examination of the specificity of the author's own environment—the component that stands at the center of Goldmann's cultural and literary studies. Thus the attachment of a structuralist component to a sociological apparatus capable of probing the specificities of societal relationships of narrative, ameliorates the shortcomings of each mode taken in isolation, and moves a long stride forward toward the establishment of a socio-poetic model which would work through the immanence of structure to mediation.

Modern models for literary analysis abound. The one I employ is uncomplicated and effective. My choice is based on its ability to deal with narrative syntax. Emphasis on this particular level is based on several factors. The most important is my contention that syntactical as well as semantic relationships are meaning-bearing in fiction. For this reason a study of a given work's narrative syntax, both at the level of its disposition as *histoire,* and *discours*, will elucidate the homologous relationship that exists between each of them and the world view of the collective subject in which the author and his thought are inscribed. This desire to stay as close as possible to the syntactical organization of the text stems from the Goldmannian substrata of my methodological assertions. It is at this level that the analysis remains closest to the sense of aesthetic organization expressed by Goldmann.

Those analytical devices that provide the tools necessary for explaining narrative structure rely primarily on the works of two theoreticians closely identified with the advances that Russian Formalism and French Structuralism have brought to modern poetics: Tzvetan Todorov and Gérard Genette. The method of narrative segmentation utilized by the former in *Grammaire du Décameron* (The Hague: Mouton, 1969) provides the basis for my isolation, quantification, and analysis of the text's *histoire*[15] His model has been altered to assimilate several of the simplifications suggested by John Rutherford in an important article published several years ago.[16] The most substantial of these modifications is the reduction of all of Todorov's verbal actions to a single category, as Rutherford believes there is one fundamental type of action without which the *histoire* cannot exist. This consists of "...the modification, or attempted or perspective modification, of a situation which affects personages in some significant way; that is

---

15. Other methods for quantification, especially in reference to arriving at a paraphrase of the action, exist. The best is the one proposed by William O. Hendricks: "Methodology of Narrative Structuralist Analysis," in his *Essays on Semio-Linguistics and Verbal Art* (The Hague: Mouton, 1973), pp. 175-195. His system, nevertheless, is unwieldy when applied to longer works, and ones in which psychological aspects as opposed to action are emphasized.

16. "Story, Character, Setting, and Narrative in Galdos' *El amigo Manso,"* in *Style and Structure in Literature. Essays in the New Stylistics*, ed. Roger Fowler (Ithaca, New York: Cornell University Press, 1975), pp. 177-212.

to say, which they regard as being either disagreeable or undesirable" (p. 186).

Rutherford also sees Todorov's definition of a sequence as uncertain, and therefore makes another change, defining it as a unitary process consisting of three propositions (here labeled A, B, and C) out of which action develops in three dialectical stages: an initial situation, an action which modifies or attempts to modify that situation, and the new situation resulting from one and two. An *histoire* may consist of any number of these sequences. I maintain Todorov's and Rutherford's way of marking the links between propositions, although I write out the components instead of using the analytical shorthand they do. Thus temporal links between propositions are shown with a plus sign ($+$) and causal relationships (resulting from attempted or successful modifications) are shown with arrows ($\rightarrow$).

At the level of textual comprehension, analysis begins with a localization and description of the main actors and sequences of the *histoire*, and the multiple interrelationships among the latter. In accordance with the goals of the model I propose, the results garnered from Todorovian operations must be carried one step further so as to demonstrate the way in which the structure of sequences is homologous to the world view of the collective subject that informs the work, thus (1) revealing the ideological message underlying the narrative arrangement of this particular aspect of narrative, and (2) helping to concretize the text/context relationship at the explanative level.

The study of *discours* and of the *histoire*'s manifestation therein conforms to the categories set forth by Genette in "Discours du récit," which occupies the major portion of *Figures III* (Paris: Seuil, 1972).[17] This is to my mind the most lucid critical model now available for dealing with these aspects of narrative form.[18] How the abstract *histoire* is

17. An English version was recently published: *Narrative Discourse. An Essay in Method,* trans. Jane E. Lewin (Ithaca, New York: Cornell University Press, 1980).

18. One possible area of difficulty is that Genette employs a three part segmentation of narrative units as opposed to the standard two inherited from Russian Formalism.

manifested in the *discours'* and how both are transmitted to the reader are studied in accordance with the tripartite division that Genette develops: *temps, mode,* and *voix,* which correspond to the three-part division of structure discussed in the previous note.

Ordre, dureé, and *fréquence,* sub-divisions of the first category, are important for the syntactical arrangements of the text for they indicate how the propositions and sequences of the *histoire* are actualized in the *discours.* Since it is concerned with the way the one-to-one correspondence between the events narrated in the *histoire* and their presentation in the *discours* is altered, *ordre* is the most important analytical category at the strictly syntagmatic level. Fundamental are the *anachronies* or disjunctions of the normal temporalogical progression that provides flashforwards to parts of the actions not yet introduced (*prolepses*) or flashbacks to material already covered or to actions that pre-date the *histoire*'s main time frame (*analepses*).

The various terms are succinctly described by Robert Scholes in his primer *Structuralism in Literature. An Introduction* (New Haven: Yale University Press, 1974).

> In their writings on fiction the formalits employ a distinction between two aspects of narrative: story (*fable*) and plot (*sujet*). The *story* is the raw material of narrative, that is, the events in their chronological sequence. The *plot* is the narrative as actually shaped. We can think of the story as being analogous to the facts of history itself, always running on the same speed, in the same direction. In a *plot,* the speed may be changed, the direction reversed, at will. Actually, a *story* always represents items selected according to some elementary law of narrative logic which eliminates irrelevancies. And a *plot* is then a further refinement which organizes these items for maximum emotional effect and thematic interest. But it is fair to say that the facts of life are to history as the story is to the plot. History selects and arranges the events of the *récit* and is similar to the Russian formalist' distinction between story and plot (*fable* and *sujet*). But there are differencës. For the formalists' story and plot are both abstractions—they are simply two arrangements of the same events—one chronological and one motivated. But for Genette only story is an abstraction. The *récit* is real. It is the words on the page, from which we readers reconstruct both story and narration. The *récit* narrated by Odysseus is contained within the *Odyssey,* a *récit* narrated by Homer (164-165).

This distinction between a two and three-part division of narrative does not really pose any difficulties. Genette's concepts of *récit* and *narration* can both be easily collapsed into what I have labeled *discours,* since *narration* is, in effect, the agency of transmission and *récit* its resultant product.

Durée is that category through which the narrative's rhythm is measured. As such it is concerned with charting the accelerations and decelerations of the artificial *discours* time (measured in the text as the physical space it occupies) relative to the *histoire* time. *Fréquence* is the least attended aspect of modern narratological studies. It measures the relationship between the repetition of events in the *histoire*, and the repetition of their presentation in the *discours*.

While not as directly related to the textual organization as the categories grouped under the heading of *temps, mode* and *voix* are vitally important to my analysis, because they regulate and focus the reader's perception of the text, and serve to emphasize the message underlying syntagmatic arrangement. The first of these, *mode*, is grouped into two sub-components, distance and perspective (*focalisations*, as Genette labels the latter), which control the narrative information presented to the reader. *Voix* is not concerned with the eyes through which the narrative is perceived, but with the speaking voice transmitting that information.[19] The central issue examined here is the actual production of the *discours*, what Genette calls *l'instance narrative*. A consideration of this critical moment encompasses not only the relationships between the events and their elaboration in the *discours*,

---

19. Genette's splitting of the one who sees in fiction (*mode*) from the one who speaks (*voix*) represents a break with traditional point of view studies. The importance of this move is discussed by Scholes in his book cited in the previous note.

    Genette's separation of voice and mood breaks the question of point-of-view in half, and in a very fruitful way. There is a great difference between the question of mood (Who sees?) and the question of voice (Who speaks?), and this difference is perpetually obscured by our traditional way of designating fictional viewpoint according to speech (first persons, etc.) or according to visions (limited, omniscient, etc.). In the study of narration we need to attend to both the question of perspective (whose vision, how limited, when shifted) and the question of voice (whose expression, how adquate, how reliable). In *The Ambassadors*, the eyes are the eyes of Strether, but the voice is the voice of James, though sometimes modulating toward Strether's. In the *Recherche*, on the other hand, the voice is the voice of Marcel, and the eyes too, are his, but both voice and eyes are so heightened by Proust himself that the perspective is at once limited (internally focused, Genette would say) and extended (externally focused), and the voice is both that of a character (internal) and that of an external narrator (p. 166-167).

but also those that exist between both of them and the *narration:* the narrative act that generates the *discours* itself.[20] *Voix* is sub-divided into several compartments, the most important of which are *temps de la narration, niveau narrative* and *personne*. The link between all of the above and the actual or virtual recipient or receptor of the narration is treated under the heading of *narrataire*.

Once the arrangement of the *discours* and the structure through which it is transmitted is delineated I go one step beyond description that structuralist and formalist criticism does not take, so as to attempt to uncover the homologous relationship between the structure of the *discours* and the mental structures of the collective subject whose world view both mediates the production of the text and is materialized in that narrative. With this, operations at both levels of narrative arrangement have been completed and the resultant narrative structures extracted from those operations at Goldmann's comprehensive level have been inserted and interpreted as the explanative level through the medium of the agent that links them: Goldmann's category of homology. One type of analysis of the text still remains: a consideration of intertextuality.

Although intertextual analysis is more closely related to paradigmatic concerns than syntagmatic ones, my model provides for its inclusion. While acknowledging the theoretical grounding of this concept in the works of Kristeva and Bakhtin, to name only two, my own utilization of it stays much closer to the definition afforded by Walter Mignolo in a recent study.[21] There he categorizes the nature of the intertextual dialogue in the following manner.

20. Genette believes that few, it any, critics have made the effort to respect the autonomy or importance of *l'instance narrative*, and that most continue to confuse it with the moment when the writer physically produced the text. This problem is discussed in depth on page 226 of his important monograph.

21. "La noción de competencia en poética," *Cuadernos Hispanoamericanos*, No. 300 (June 1975), pp. 605-622. An indication of the increasing attention that intertextuality is receiving in critical circles is that two important journals, *New York Review* and *Poétique*, have both devoted monographic numbers to this topic. Another important study recently appeared in *Romanic Review*. I refer to Gustavo Pérez Firmat's "Apuntes para un modelo de la intertextualidad en literatura," 79 (1978), 1-19.

Estos aspectos aparecen si se asume que todo texto poético es dialógico en relación con otros textos. Es común, como ejemplo simple, ver en las novelas policiales referencias a otras novelas policiales. Un texto como *Cobra* de Severo Sarduy está conscientemente construido en relación a otros textos. Los ejemplos pueden multiplicarse. Claro está que el lector puede leer y comprender *Cobra* según los mecanismos que podrían ser descritos por GF, GT y GP prescindiendo de las relaciones con otros textos. Su lectura se modificará según que el lector tenga o no adquirido este tipo de competencia que llamaremos intertextual. La intertextualidad no es sólo relación de textos poéticos, sino también de texto poético y lengua cotidiana (p. 617-618).

Of fundamental importance in this appraisal is the assertion that a knowledge of the dialogic nature of the text is a function of the reader's literary competence. The identification of the links between texts (whether overtly established or not) widens the scope of its possible readings. Admission of such an analytical mechanism is a function both of the type of literature under study here, and the repressive conditions under which it was produced. Such circumstances tend to generate texts part of whose message is tied to the readers' competence to provide expanding parameters of interpretation through the recognition of intertextual keys. Prevailing conditions provide for the ideological exploitation of intertextual links overtly established by the author, and directed to a reader with the competence to perceive both the link and its intention. In this way intertextual analysis also serves to underscore the meaning behind structure, by emphasizing the ideological message imbedded in the narrative's syntactical disposition.[22]

---

22. Just such an intertextual study comprises Chapter IV of this monograph: "Juan Benet's Intertextual Web," which demonstrates how the novelist exploits the link he establishes with Sir James Frazer's *The Golden Bough.* I treat the intertextual link between Benet and the Brazilian author Euclides da Cunha in "Región's Brazilian and Backlands: The Link between *Volverás a Región* and Euclides da Cunha's *Os Sertões," Hispanic Journal* 1, No. 2 (Spring, 1980), 25-45.

The working of the methodology I propose will be demonstrated through an analysis, as indicated above, of *Volverás a Región* (Barcelona: Destino, 1967), perhaps the most taxing presentation of the Spanish Civil War and its effects produced in francoist Spain. My choice of this particular text is based on its recognized artistic merit and decidedly complex organization. This second aspect is of considerable importance for, as I noted previously, many of the studies of this novel perceive no ideological intent in its presentation of the Civil War. For this reason its study is doubly interesting. It provides me with the opportunity to test my sociologically oriented model with a highly complex narrative, and the chance to demonstrate the shortcomings of other approaches to such fiction that are not equipped to appraise the relationships between narrative form and meaning.

CHAPTER II

Juan Benet in Context

I
Juan Benet in Post-War Fiction

Juan Benet Goitia was born in 1927 in Madrid. His father died in the first days of the Civil War, and thus Benet's life, like that of so many other Spaniards, was personally marked by an historical event that was to have a profound effect on his psyche.[1] After the war he completed his *bachillerato* in Madrid, and subsequently studied in the Escuela de Ingenieros de Caminos y Puertos. Upon finishing his studies he spent the period between 1954 and 1964 away from the capital working on various public works projects, many in northeast Spain. Although his academic training was scientific and technical, he always had a pronounced literary avocation and frequented a number of important literary or culturally oriented *tertulias* such as the one held in the apartment of Pío Baroja, and those at the Gambrinus restaurant and the Café Gijón.[2]

1. A comment made during the interview wich Antonio Núñez, "Encuentro con Juan Benet", that appeared in *Insula*, No. 269 (April, 1969), 4 is of importance in this respect. Asked by the interviewer "¿Cómo transcurrió tu infancia y tu adolescencia?" Benet responded as follows: "Creo que lo que más me influyó fue la guerra civil, que me sorprendió a los nueve años: verse separado de los padres, vivir las dos Españas y, por una de esas paradojas de la vida, desfilar en Madrid con los pioneros de Lenin y ver en San Sebastián el desfile de los falangistas que habían conquistado Calpe. Las circunstancias de la guerra asoman en mis dos novelas, más en la primera". Barbara Probst Solomon's autobiographical novel *Arriving Where We Started"* (New York: Harper and Row, 1972) provides interesting background information on Benet and his family. Its Spanish translation appeared as *Los felices cuarenta: una educación sentimental* (Barcelona: Seix Barral, 1978).

2. Alfonso Sastre, in his informative essay "Poco más que anéccdotas 'culturales' alrededor de quince años (1950-1965)," *Triunfo,* Número Extraordinario No. 507, 17

While he had published several pieces earlier, it was as the 1960's drew too a close that Benet began to publish seriously in the field of fiction and essay, and he has become, indubitably, the most important writer to emerge in Spain in the 1970's.[3] Highly talented, better read than almost all his contemporaries, Benet is prone to make polemical and iconoclastic statements both in print and during public appearances. These attributes, coupled with the highly complex and seemingly impenetrable narrative discourse he writes, have helped to produce a type of enigmatic aura surrounding his person and a critical furor, partly sparked by serious misconceptions, around his work. Recognized by many to be in the vanguard of the "new" Spanish literature that emerged in the 1970's the writer has also been hailed as the most important novelist to appear in Spain since the death of Luis Martín-Santos (coincidentally a close friend of Benet), and *Volverás a Región*, his most important novel, is numbered with *Recuento* by Luis Goytisolo, *Reivindicación del conde don Julián* by Juan Goytisolo, and Martín-Santos' *Tiempo de silencio* among the four most important narratives produced in recent years in Spain.[4]

Less than positive assessments also exist. Benet has been characterized as an elitist author whose narrative talents begin to slide after his first two novels.[5] His work has been criticized for being part of an

June, 1972, offers the following interesting comments on the Gambrinus *tertulia*. "Aquellos de 'Gambrinus' era una tertulia muy seria, nuestro vínculo con ellos — Miguel Sánchez Mazas, Eva Forest, los citados-Benet-Martín Santos, Sánchez de Zavala y otros— se esblecía ocasionalmente, sobre todo a través de Francisco Pérez Navarro, que a mi modo de ver, estudiaba con ellos y prefería divertirse con nosotros" (p. 84).

3. In addition to his well-known narrative and essayistic production, Benet has also authored several plays and some poetry. These works are listed in my "Juan Benet and His Critics," *Anales de la Novela de Posguerra*, 3 (1978), 123-141.

4. See Pere Gimferrer "El pensamiento literario (1939-1976)," in *La cultura bajo el franquismo*, ed. José María Castellet. (Barcelona: Ediciones de Bolsillo, 1977), pp. 105-130. The bibliographic essay mentioned in the previous note contains a fairly exhaustive bibliography of Benet criticism. An expanded and up-dated version of that essay will appear in a collection of essays on Benet and his work that is now in press.

5. Darío Villanueva, "La novela de Juan Benet," *Camp de L'Arpa*, No. 8 (November 1973), pp. 9-16.

anti-realist *contraola* that is nothing more than a carbon copy of the French *nouveau roman*.[6] Others have equated Benet's apparent turning away from the kind of portrayal of Spain's social ills that was the main component of neo-realist aesthetics with an ethical ambivalence and tacit support of the reactionary ideology of the francoist regime.[7]

The constant underlying all such divergent opinions is the perception of a Benet in the forefront of a literary vanguard, or a figure who represents an alternative distinct from what preceded him.[8] Characterizations of this nature can be somewhat misleading. Benet needs to be placed within the parameters of the broad literary trajectory described by the narrative evolution of the Generation of 1950 to which he belongs by reasons of age, personal affinities, friendships, and literary values. I therefore agree with José Ortega's assertions in a study on the novelist's work.[9]

Una breve ubicación literaria de Benet nos ayudará a una mejor apreciación de las coordenadas histórico-culturales en que se mueve este autor. El realismo crítico-social de los componentes de la generación de medio siglo, es decir, aquellos escritores nacidos

6. José Corrales Egea, *La novela española actual: ensayo de ordenación*, (Madrid: Cuadernos para el Diálogo, 1971). See especially Chapter 10: "La 'contraola' y la liquidación del realismo," pp. 191-225.

7. Two articles by Isaac Montero are the most strident in this type of attack. I refer to "Acotaciones a una mesa redonda: respuestas a Juan Benet y defensa apresurada del realismo," *Cuadernos para el Diálogo*, Número Extra 23 (December 1970), pp. 65-74 and "La novela española de 1955 hasta hoy: una crisis de dos exaltaciones antagónicas," *Triunfo*, Número Extra 507 (17 June 1972), pp. 86-94. In the second article Montero also accused Benet of being only a carbon copy of Faulkner.

8. In "Sobre Juan Benet," *Plural: Revista Mensual de Excelsior,"* No. 17 (February 1973), pp. 13-16, Pere Gimferrer states that Benet is the novelist who has had the most impact on the development of younger Spanish writers. Information provided by those authors in two collections of interviews, Fernando Tola de Habich's *Los españoles y el boom* (Caracas: Editorial Tiempo Nuevo, 1971), and Federico Campbell's *Infame Turba* (Barcelona: Lumen, 1971), corroborates Gimferrer's view.

9. José Ortega, "Estudios sobre la obra de Juan Benet," *Cuadernos Hispanoamericanos*, No. 284 (February 1974), pp. 229-258.
37

entre 1925-1935, cuya obra empieza a aparecer en la década de los cincuenta, pierde vigencia en la primera parte de los sesenta por la imposibilidad del esperado cambio de las estructuras socio-económicas españolas. Esta nueva toma de conciencia proyecta al escritor de la generación de 1950 (J. Goytisolo, A. Ferres, García Hortelano, etc.) a la exploración de orbes inter-subjectivos mediante la impugnación y superación del pasado instrumento literario. De un naturalismo basado en las motivaciones y acciones del hombre externo, se pasa a la existencia psíquica, al hombre interno. La actitud de estos escritores obedece, pues, a los condicionamientos históricos del país que provocaron, como hemos dicho, el abandono de una literatura de denuncia, 'la antiestética', en favor de una narrativa basada en la búsqueda del sentido de la personalidad humana, ahondada en el fondo del caos, donde subjetividad y objetividad han desaparecido.

La prolongada estancia de algunos de estos autores (J. Goytisolo, Ferres, López Pacheco, etc.) en el extranjero ha enriquecido, por la integración cultural a que el escritor se ve obligado, la cosmovisión del hombre y de los modelos expresivos que trasladan esta experiencia vital. No es, pues, un afán innovador lo que caracteriza esta *contraola* integrada por los así llamados *novísimos*, sino una nueva forma de apropiación de la realidad determinada por la subversión de valores que han condenado al hombre de fines del siglo XX a una radical incomunicación y exposesión. El escritor de la generación de medio siglo, sin abandonar el compromiso social con su momento histórico, ha encausado sus modos expresivos hacia el compromiso con el lenguaje y con el minoritario grupo de lectores a los cuales se le exige una cooperación y participación total en la lectura-creación de la obra (pp. 229-230).

This change is also evident in those writers of previous generations whose works demonstrate the most concern for Spain's problems. Important manifestations of this tendency can be found in recent works by Cela such as *San Camilo, 1936*, and Delibes, *Cinco horas con Mario, Parábola del náufrago, Las guerras de nuestros antepasados*.

Thus it is in the best writers of the first two post war generations of novelists that one can see the fundamental turn serious Spanish narrative takes. From a straightforward denunciation of social ills couched in the language, style and structure of neo-realism or behaviorism, authors evolve toward a more complex literary discourse where the properties of aesthetic organization have as important a role in the construction of that text's meaning as does its content. Such an evolution, as Ortega righfully points out, does not signal an abrogation of socially critical intent, only a reorientation of how to express that disaccord with the socio-political situation in francoist Spain.

It is my contention that Juan Benet needs to be placed within this broad ideological grouping of authors opposed to the regime, and that the ordering process attesting to his affinities with the world view of that collective subject are found in *Volverás a Región*. On the surface such assertions seem slightly outlandish since most assessments of Benet wish to demonstrate his isolation from the political realities of Franco's Spain, and most essays on *Volverás a Región* either downplay the importance of the vision of the Civil War presented therein, or find it to be an ecumenical treatment of the kind described in chapter one of this study.

In the succeeding sections of this chapter I will address myself to the first of these considerations by analyzing Juan Benet's comments and essays on Spanish literature and the socio-cultural ambience of francoist Spain. This exposition serves dual functions. It is vital to my analysis of the world view mediating *Volverás a Región*, since one would hope to find in Benet's essayistic production some indication of the anti-regime sentiment underlying his narrative. Ancillary to the immediate goal of this study, but of interest to Benet scholarship in general, is the fact that the majority of the material I will examine in subsequent pages has been overlooked by critics more interested in his theoretical writings or his fiction. Filling this lacuna is a necessity because on many occasions Benet has been chastized for statements that appear outlandish when viewed in isolation but which take on an internal coherence when scrutinized as a well-defined, albeit polemical, whole. Additionally, it allows for a closer look at Benet's view of contemporary Spanish fiction, one which corroborates my assertions that the narrative project he has carried out describes an arc whose trajectory is the same as the one followed by writers such as Juan and Luis Goytisolo.

The manifestation of the world view of the anti-regime collective subject in the aesthetic organization of *Volverás a Región* is analyzed in chapters three and four of this monograph.

II

Juan Benet and Spain

Literature

Benet's views on Spanish literature are underscored by a clearly-defined, though polemical body of theoretical views that have been discussed elsewhere.[10] While the primary emphasis here will be on the opinions he has expressed on the post-war novel, it is worth-while to present in a synoptic manner his views on earlier periods of Spanish literature so as to point out the breadth of Benet's knowledge of his own literary heritage. This is not to say that I agree with the ideas expressed in the essays to be examined. But contrary to some critics, I see an internal coherence in his literary pronouncements.

---

10. A number of studies on this subject exist. The first major assessment of Benet's theory can be found in David Herzberger's *The Novelistic World of Juan Benet* (Clear Creek, Indiana: The American Hispanist, 1977). Recent studies have added substantially to the important information contained in Herzberger's chapter on Benet's theory. See especially Herzberger's "Theoretical Approaches to the Spanish New Novel: Juan Benet and Juan Goytisolo," *Revista de Estudios Hispánicos*, 14, No. 2 (May 1980), 3-17; Diego Martínez Torrón's "Juan Benet o los márgenes de la sorpresa," in Juan Benet, *Un viaje de invierno*, ed. Diego Martínez Torrón (Madrid: Cátedra, 1980), pp. 11-110 (see especially pp. 46-60); and Jorge Rodríguez Padrón's "Apuntes para una teoría benetiana," *Insula*, Nos. 396-397 (November-December 1979), pp. 3,5. My "The Paradoxes of Praxis: Juan Benet and Modern Poetics," now in press treats aspects of Benet's theoretical discourse not previously addressed. Herzberger's "Enigma as Narrative Determinant in Juan Benet," *Hispanic Review*, 49 (1979), 149-157 shows how enigma, a pivotal component in Benet's essayistic prose, is embodied in his fiction.

Pivotal to his examination of Spanish literature is a meditation of the causes behind the disappearance of what he labels the grand style.

En este libro traté de indagar la razón por la cual despareció del castellano el *grand style* para dar paso al costumbrismo. Supongo que la razón es muy compleja y controvertible; pero el hecho está ahí y los clásicos castellanos relegados a la universidad. Con frecuencia se piensa que el *grand style* era el precio más barato para obtener el *Quijote*, una pieza que vale por todo lo demás y que justifica toda la mediocridad que le circunda. Semejante manera de pensar, más propia para la Bolsa que para la Academia, no es más que un ardid un tanto turbio para menospreciar la pérdida. ¿Porqué hasta qué punto un estilo literario para ser vigente y nacional tiene que ser monopolista? ¿Es que Racine desplazó a Molière? ¿Es que alguien en París llegó a considerarlos incompatibles? En nuestro país al parecer sí, a juzgar por las muestras que nos han llegado y que han venido a demostrar, por el lado más inofensivo y gratuito, nuestra acreditada tendencia a la intolerancia.

La vida del intolerante es miserable, engañosa y sórdida, lo mismo para el individuo que para el estilo. Y aquella afición que se apoderó del país, más o menos contemporánea con la llegada de los Borbones, se había de conformar con unas letras que —para el gusto moderno— tienen más de empachosas que de otra cosa. Tal vez la falta de verdadero alimento fue lo que redujo nuestro estómomago, lo que hace que nuestro cuerpo colectivo tolere mal los platos fuertes.[11]

The disappearance to which Benet refers begins in the sixteenth century. From that date forward he isolates two antithetical but interrelated tendencies in Spanish letters that will eventually lead to *costumbrismo*'s virtual monopoly on Spanish literature.[12] The grand style

11. *La inspiración y el estilo*, 2nd ed. (Barcelona: Seix Barral, 1974) p. 10.
12. *Costumbrismo* as explained in *La inspiración y el estilo* is a literary mode that

to which Benet refers was taken up by what the novelist labels "la España oficial" for use in the instigation of the "heroic" political ventures the Spanish crown was undertaking. The problem with this type of literature was twofold: it was serving imperial political ends for which the Spanish people had little taste, and in which they had little faith. Secondly, being official, this body of literature was almost devoid of inspiration and intrinsic artistic merit. "Toda la literatura heróica española desde Ercilla hasta Quintana o Pemán, no es por esa razón más que un altar a los convencionalismos, a las verdades dictadas por la autoridad competente, tan falto de vigor, tan carente de inspiración que hasta los hispanistas más celosos han preferido olvidarse de ella para cargar el acento sobre las glorias inaccesibles de nuestro casticismo" (*Inspiración*, pp. 96-97). In addition to producing a countercurrent in literature the heroic initiative on the part of the monarchy also produced a tremendous shock in the soul of Spain's people.

Un pueblo que no tenía fe en las grandes aventuras políticas y espirituales que le impusieron sus gobernantes y que, en consecuencia, tuvo que sufrir una de esas sacudidas medulares con que, si quieres como si no quieres, el Estado decide despertar la conciencia del país y apoderarse de ella para sus propios fines y que —lo hemos venido a comprobar palmariamente en el siglo XX— el pueblo tiene que aceptar sin rechistar, inconsciente de la transformación que se va a operar en su propia conciencia (*Inspiración*, p. 96).

Based as it was on a project in which the people put little hope, and poorly written, this literature produced nothing but scorn on the part of writers and the general public. It therefore became the object of ridicule of other writers who saw through the sham. But since it was *official*, supportive of the state and supported by it, those bent on ridiculing this literature could vent their sarcasm on everthing except the true object of their scorn: the state itself. Since censorship made it

attempts a critical assessment of its own ambience through a faithful portrayal of the surface manifestations of that reality. It fails because it delves no deeper than the surface, and is condemned precisely because its artistic elaboration of the material it treats is suspect.

impossible for them to attack the state, they released their ire on what Benet labels the "prototipos del estado llano".

> Y sucedió lo que tenía que suceder: el sentido crítico del país, su sentido de ridículo, su aversión al arte "pompier" y su ansia de supervivencia y preservación de las virtudes nacionales vinieron a aunarse en secreto contra un disfraz que no le convenía y contra el que era preciso, por un procedimiento metafórico, irónico y simulado, montar un unánime proceso de burla y desenmarcamiento. Como objeto de burla podía servir cualquier cosa —salvo el propio Estado defendido por la censura— que a través de una conducta impersonal, autoritaria, ridícula, inoportuna e impertinente se emparentara con la representación física de la máquina estatal. Y para burlarse de él no hacía sino recurrir a cualquiera de los prototipos del estado llano, los golfillos, los buscavidas, los aventureros (*Inspiración*, p. 97).

Literally this led to a ridiculing of the grand style, since it was now identified with a state-motivated project of heroic proportions which in turn generated its own literary works to support political goals. "En cuanto al gran estilo no le cupo otra cosa que el ser ridiculizado en público. A partir del mismo siglo todas las referencias a la gran tradición que informa siempre ese estilo son siempre burlescas" (*Inspiración*, p. 97). This reaction first engenders what Benet labels "castismo" and lack of "compenetración" with his country caused by authorial dissatisfaction, which explains, in turn, why Spain has no figures who are totally integrated in their country's collective projects.[13]

---

13. Yo no veo en el horizonte de nuestras letras ningún Schiller, ningún Miltón, ningún Kleist, ni un Stendhal ni un Tolstoi, esos hombres que —cualquiera que sea su estatura artística— parecen siempre fundidos en una sociedad y compenetrados con una aventura colectiva de la que extrajeron la mejor inspiración para cantar lo único que merecía un verdadero respeto. Ni siquiera veo, a partir del siglo XVI, un espíritu semejante del que informó el *Cantar de Mío Cid*, o las *Coplas* de Jorge Manrique. Veo —en contraste— un interminable desfile de figuras agazapadas, profesionales del sarcasmo y el descontento, maestros incomparables de la metáfora, de la elipses o de la obrepción, que se han acostumbrado a vivir en un estado de sorna clandestina porque el verdadero objeto de su furor, el Estado, fue siempre tabú

The artist's sense of alienation leads to the great stylistic change Benet describes. The grand style, because of its inextricable link with officialdom, and the inefficacious way in which such literature was produced, forces the artist to turn his back on this style and precipitates what Benet describes as Spanish literature's "entrada en la taberna." In time, the turning away from the grand style engenderse, the morally and didactically correct, but artistically impoverished, production of the eighteenth and nineteenth centuries which culminates in what for the Spanish writer is the height of mediocrity: the realistic and naturalistic novel of the nineteenth century whose roots are firmly planted in the *costumbrista* tradition. Long after the concrete reasons for this movement away from the grand style disappeared, it was nonetheless the same decidedly *castizo* and critical style that would serve as the model for eighteenth and nineteenth-century writers. Unaware of the original reasons that precipitated the grand style's displacement by a more *castizo* artistic idiom, writers of the later period nevertheless employed that *castizo* form to voice their own discontent with the Spanish situation of their own era.

In the eighteenth century this *afán docente* that overcomes literature triggers the production of works whose aim was to reform Spain. What the writers of those works failed to take into consideration, Benet argues, is that social goals need to have at their disposal a literary language capable of persuading, in additon to good intentions.

The literature of the following century would only confuse matters more. Thinking themselves innovators, Spanish and European authors would come to consider naturalism a new literary form. But for Benet its roots were in the sixteenth century. What is more, the

para ellos. En sus manos, el gran estilo (y la tradición clásica) no cumplió otra función que la de desviar el resentimiento hacia el estado y transformarlo, por la vía del menosprecio, en una actitud estética. Semejante estado de espíritu no podía conducir sino al casticismo, una manera que se ha interpretado —y valorado— como la más genuina manifestación de la fibra nacional y que en definitiva, desde Cervantes a Larra, desde Quevedo a Unamuno, más significa una perversión, una desviación y una inhibición que una actitud conforme a un apetito natural y a un espíritu sincero (*Inspiración*, pp. 101-102).

new form that the naturalists created, while morally and sociologically sound, was devoid of creative talent.

Benet's most systematic attack on the literature of the nineteenth century, and one of his most polemical essays, is his piece on Galdós published in *Cuadernos para el Diálogo*.[14] Admittedly combative, the opinions expressed therein are in total accord with the writer's own view of literature. According to Benet, Galdós has been lionized because liberal Spanish intellectuals of later generations have created a place for him in Spanish literature based not on the quality of his art but his posîtion as a champion of liberal causes.

Obviously Benet is wrong in his appraisal of the inherent artistic value of Galdós work, and Galdós' reputation cannot be attributed only to his position as a liberal crusader. Yet Benet's statements about Galdós are the logical consequence of his literary views. For Benet the most important force in literature is the creative talent of the artist manifested in his style. Coupled with this is the twentieth-century writer's distase for literary studies that do not have as their base the artistic merits of literary production. Since he sees no artistic merit in Galdós' production, and he believes that the nineteenth-century novelist's reputation is founded on the kind of literary studies he deplores, it would be highly unlikely to expect any type of opinion other than that voiced in the *Cuadernos para el Diálogo* article.

Also chastized are Galdós' champions: Spanish liberal intellectuals, dubbed the *izquierda española*.[15] Benet's literary sensibility

---

14. "Reflexiones sobre Galdós," *Cuadernos para el Diálogo*, Número Extra. 23 (December 1970), pp. 13-15.

15. A la izquierda española nunca le importó gran cosa que el instrumento artístico de Galdós fuera de punta gruesa. A la izquierda española (cuando no sospecha de todo instrumento de punta fina como un útil que sirve a la reacción) eso le trae un tanto sin cuidado porque entiende que —desde hace muchos años— la literatura española es, toda ella, cosa suya. Y eso debe ser así no tanto porque los profesores de letras acostumbran ser de izquierda —salvo raras excepciones, especialmente especialistas en Lope o la novela cántabra—, sino porque la derecha no escribe. Los últimos vestigios de aquella extraña raza de hombres que con su pluma defendieron la causa de la derecha demostraba más pudor para reconocerlo así —e incluso se atrevía a entrar en polémica para hacer acto de presencia en la sociedad docta—; fue

makes him wary of trends and modes. Moreover, he holds that the stylistic tyranny that characterized earlier periods carries over into post-war Spain where it is the leftist-leaning intellectuals who control the literary establishment and effectively monopolize it with their socially-minded narrative. The latter has the same drawbacks and deficiencies found in eighteenth and nineteenth-century literature: a lack of inherent artistic merit. What is more, they attacked all those who disagreed with them, and, for a period of years, blocked any attempt to open new trends in Spanish fiction.[16]

Benet has not written extensively on twentieth-century Spanish literature. Most of his statements arise precisely because as a successful practicing novelist this is a subject that interviews always broach, or one on which he is frequently asked to lecture.[17] A notable exception is the article "Barojiana," published in the book by the same name (Madrid: Taurus, 1972). This essay provides Benet's very personal opinions on don Pío and sheds valuable light on the statement made in his interview with Campbell in *Infame Turba* in which the writer admitted that "--De los españoles modernos el único que me interesa es Pío Baroja" (p. 195)[18] Benet's reminiscences of the time spent at the

alrededor de esos años cuando reconoció que debía conformarse con tener en sus manos las riendas del poder, sin preocuparse de defender nada con la palabra y cediendo gustosa a la izquierda la poca satisfacción y dinero que se extrae con el ejercicio de las letras. (De la regla anterior existe —es natural— una excepción: la de las así llamadas letras que dan dinero y que continúan en manos de la derecha. Pero como eso más que un tema literario es un negocio, todavía no sé de nadie solvente que considere oportuno ocuparse de ellas ("Reflexiones sobre Galdós", p. 14).

16. Benet's position regarding the *izquierda literaria* is not as negative as it appears to be here. While opposed to the artistic tyranny that this group maintained over Spanish letters, he shared their demonstrated critical intent vis-à-vis froncoism and their desire to see this institution disappear.

17. The solicitation of Benet as a lecturer both inside Spain and abroad is the surest sign of his ever-increasing recognition as one of his country's most important practicing novelits. The revised version of my bibliographic essay on the novelist (see n. 4) cites many such speaking engagements.

18. A strictly literary reason for his predilection for Baroja's narrative can be found in other of Benet's essays. I refer to the author's professed affection for the adventure novel evident in "Algo acerca del buque fantasma," *La inspiración* pp. 141-154.

Baroja *tertulia* help to explain the reasons behind the previous statement. "Baroja es el mejor altavoz de toda la ridiculez de cierta retórica castellana, sobre todo la de sus contemporáneos, el más riguroso patrón con el que medir las ínfulas de la época moderna, el Fiel Contraste de la novela española del siglo XX; y tal vez, también el tronco del que tendrán que partir algunas ramas de la narrativa que él mismo podó" ("Barojiana," p. 39). What Benet finds attractive in don Pío is that he mirrors Benet's own iconoclastic spirit. Moreover Benet fails to see in the Basque novelist the same shortcomings perceived in other modern Spanish writers. While he does not hold up Baroja as a model for future Spanish novelists, he states that Spanish writers will have to take account of Baroja's work when contemplating a literary vocation.[19]

Benet's admiration of Baroja's iconoclastic nature transcends literature, and is bound up with the social and political opinions he was exposed to at the *tertulia*. In short, it is a function of what he believes Baroja stands for. Indicative of this is his description of a journalist's attempts to inteview Baroja. This representative of the strictly controlled Spanish press was determined to get the Basque author to admit how well life was going for him in Spain, something the latter steadfastly refused to do. As important as the description of the event itself (reproduced below) is the tone in which Benet's opinions on the Spanish ambience of the 1940's is conveyed.

En cierta ocasión todos los asistentes a la tertulia recibimos una entrevista a don Pío, tal vez con motivo de su cumpleaños; *era uno de esos hombres de catadura entusiasta, que sin duda consideraba*

Referring directly to the Basque writer, Benet states in the Núñez interview, "En este país no ha habido, yo creo que desde el siglo XIX, novela de aventuras, novela de misterio, novela de mar —excepto de Baroja—..." (p. 4).

19. "Pero lo mismo que el nuevo hombre de letras no fijara su atención en esa meta, no tendrá más remedio que volverse para mirarle; un tanto apartado del camino, intemporal, petrificado en su carácter retarido y, sin embargo, permanentemente admonitorio: advirtiendo al joven los peligros de la caducidad de todo arte y toda personalidad brillante" ("Barojiana," p. 40).

como una obligación profesional dar fe de todo lo que veía a su alre-
dedor se encontraba en una situación inmejorable. (La mentalidad
vigente nunca se liberaría de los métodos de la propaganda bélilca,
sin duda porque nunca daría por cancelada la situación de la belige-
rancia; y el más repulsivo y contagioso de sus vicios conduce al
infantilismo de repetir incansablemente las glorias de nuestro paraí-
so). Pero a medida que se sucedían las preguntas, las respuestas no
podían ser más desconsoladoras. Don Pío se quejaba de su mucha
edad, de su falta de interés por las cosas, del precio del carbón, del
frío que pasaba, del insomnio que padecía, del poco entusiasmo
que le inspiraba la calle, de lo duro que era una existencia que a su
edad le obligaba a seguir escribiendo para ganarse el sustento. No
debía ser eso lo que esperaba el periodista, poco dispuesto a servir
a sus lectores un pensamiento tan negativo por lo que, pese a las
quejas y protestas de don Pío, arreciaba con preguntas en las que
ya estaba implícita una contestación más optimista y sonriente:
"pero se encuentra usted rodeado de buenos amigos, la cabeza le
funciona a perfección, se divierte escribiendo, tiene usted una casa
confortable…" "No, nada de eso," replicaba don Pío, muy poco
satisfecho de que se pretendiera contradecir su juicio sobre su propia condición, en el que sin duda estaba implícita una actitud
moral. "Pero a fin de cuentas," —le dijo el periodista, un tanto
impaciente, deseoso de obtener, aunque fuera con una afirmación
neutra y total, lo que andaba buscando— "en general se encuentra
usted bien ¿no es así?" "No señor" —fue la terrible respuesta del
viejo— "en general me encuentro mal, bastante mal. Pero me da lo
mismo encontrarme bien que encontrarme mal" (pp. 21-22, (italics
mine)

Over and above the anecdotal interest inherent in the episode described, what stands out is Benet's admiration of Baroja's unwillingness to bend his opinion in the face of a reporter who desired
endorsement of the Franco regime. Baroja's intransigence in the
matter is illuminating since attempts were made to quote his writing
out of context so as to portray the Basque writer as supportive of the

authoritarian ideology of the francoist regime.[20] Benet's anecdote demonstrates that such attempts did not sway don Pío, and his refusal to be characterized as supportive of the government appears to have inspired Benet's admiration.

The same esteem is evident in the following citation from the same article. Here Benet sums up his reflections on Baroja's *tertulia*.

> Para mí aquel par de horas en su casa, cada diez o quince días, constituía la única posibilidad de ver con mis ojos un orden que por otras partes veía turbado; del que me habían hablado en casa pero que yo no llegaría a compartir ni disfrutar; a falta de una sociedad en la que vivir con cierto gusto, a la que prestar el propio concurso, no quedaba más que la visita devota a las ruinas de la civilización precedente y la participación en la lucha por la que clamaba mi hermano y Cirilo Benítez. Ninguna de las dos cosas existen hoy por hoy. De la segunda queda siempre la esperanza en volver a concebir la esperanza. De la primera, la imagen de una reunión de personas que —imortalizados en la luz de la tarde, con los chillidos de las golondrinas o los vencejos— al mismo tiempo que la fe han perdido toda acrimonia; incluso Julio Caro, el más vehemente, enojado y constante de todos los intransigentes (p. 42).

Both this passage and the previous one underscore the fact that Benet's fondness for the Basque writer is rooted in his identification with Baroja's unwillingness to support the government in power. That Benet characterizes the participants in the *tertulia* as "las ruinas de la civilización precedente" is highly significant given my contention that he fits within the parameters of a grouping which views francoism as having brought on a period of decadence and decay at all of societal organization. Benet's expression of admiration for the Baroja *tertulia*, then, indirectly voices his personal hostility and discomfort with the

---

20. Manuel Vázquez Montalbán points this out in his essay "La pervertida sentimentalidad de Pío Baroja," in *Barojiana*, pp. 155-176. See especially the comments on p. 156.

francoist environment. Tangentially manifested in his admiration for don Pío, these attitudes are openly vented at other times in highly negative comments about the regime. To cite one example, the underscored sections and especially the parenthetical sentence of the passage quoted above are indicative of his disagreement with the regime. The very parenthetical nature of this statement bestows upon it the quality of a personal attack on that moment's political situation by setting it apart from the body of the paragraph, and thus emphasizing its importance.

The anti-francoist sentiments articulated in the "Barojiana" article are similar to ones contained in Benet's other remarks about Franco's Spain which will be studied below. If these ideas are kept in mind when the author's opinions on contemporary Spanish fiction are examined, a substantial re-evaluation of his concept of social literature results.

The writer's critical comments on the fiction produced by his contemporaries appear to be consistent but his remarks on his knowledge of it are less so. On certain occasions he has admitted a nodding acquaintance with it. As he remarked in the Núñez interview.

"No crees que soy un experto. He leído algunos premios sonados, alguna novela que me han recomendado los amigos" (p. 4). The impression of only a cursory familiarity with contemporary fiction is strengthened in the Tola de Habich interview. When asked about the works of Cela and Delibes, the Spanish novelist replied as follows:

B: No los conozco.
—¿No ha leído nada de ellos?
B: ¿De Cela? Si, he leído algo.
—¿Ha leído *San Camilo*?
B: No
—¿Y de Delibes?
B: No sé (p. 40).

Close examination reveals, however, that Benet has read more contemporary fiction than he is willing to admit in the Tola de Habich interview. Portions of the last paragraph of his article on Galdós are very revealing in this respect.

> De esa forma el resultado no puede ser otro: el buen chico de Valladolid, un poco tímido y timorato, descontento del actual estado de las cosas, prefiere arremeter contra la ortografía antes de levantar demasiado la voz; el chulapado, descarado y castizo de Galicia resolverá el espinoso tema de la guerra civil poniendo en boca de ambos contendientes las mismas palabrotas, y el intérrimo catalán se atreverá a reprochar a sus colegas del otro lado del océano la libertad que él no disfruta, y para sobrellevar el aburrimiento de una fiesta tan fastidiosa, un público devoto —e inasequible al desaliento—, aunque escaso, cantará las grandezas de los tiempos de Galdós y Machaquito. Pero no hay que rasgarse las vestiduras: La fiesta del castellano resulta tan decepcionante como las de las provincias y países limítrofes (p. 15).

The allusions to post-war writers contained in this statement contradict the assertions Benet made in the interviews. The "buen chico de Valladolid" to whom he refers is, of course, Miguel Delibes, and the reference to "arremeter contra la ortografía" can only point to Delibes' *Parábola del náufrago* (Barcelona: Destino, 1969) in which the destruction of orthographic rules becomes a structural feature of the text. The "chulapado" from Galicia can only be Cela, and Benet's caustic comments about the Civil War refer to Cela's famous *San Camilo, 1936* (Madrid: Alfaguara, 1969). Not only has Benet read Delibes, then, something he refuses to acknowledge in the Tola de Habich interview, but he had already read a novel that was published only shortly before the interview took place. The same is true of the reference to *San Camilo, 1936*. In the interview he says he is not familiar with it, but in the essay on Galdós he makes a point of singling out this novel for criticism. Further proof of the breadth of his readings is the fact that he is willing to criticize the novels of Juan Goytisolo, "el intérrimo catalán," something, we may assume, he would not do if he were not familiar with them.

While equivocal about the extent of his knowledge of the field, Benet points out in the Campbell interview that as a practicing writer he has the responsability to make some kind of a judgment about it.

Yo estoy y sigo siendo muy al margen y no vivo de las letras y si no fuera por este desgraciado premio Biblioteca Breve, estaría mucho más al margen y ninguna persona me vendría a entrevistar. Pero los juicios que yo tengo sobre las situaciones de las que he estado al margen no quieren decir que yo me sustraiga de la responsabilidad del juicio (p. 304).

Benet's view of the post-war novel is guided by the same general literary principles underlying all his cultural judgments, and his rejection of peninsular fiction of that era is predicated on its poor quality, sociological orientation, and manifestation of the kind of literary tyranny he abhors, and which plays an important role in the Spanish cultural ambience of the period.

Benet consistently criticizes post-war fiction's poor artistic quality which emanates from its costumbristic nature. In remarks on contemporary fiction made during the Campbell interview he states, "La verdad para ser sincero, no me interesó nunca nada. Pero en mí ya viene de muy antiguo: nunca me ha interesado el costumbrismo. Y en definitiva, esa era una fórmula un poco más irritada y más solemne, pero era costumbrista. El costumbrismo en sí me ha dicho siempre muy poco" (p. 296). Dislike for the post-war novel is linked to his lack of interest in the modern Spanish novel in general, as he points out in the Núñez interview: "Creo que la novela de hoy, la de ayer y la de anteayer, es una novela que le falta imaginación y que, aceptando en cada momento el dictado moral, el escritor español no ha salido de cierto costumbrismo muy romo. Y esto, sea en la novela de estampas, en la novela de costumbres, en la novela de denuncia social, ha estado siempre limitado a un tipo de narración demasiado sujeta a la vida cotidiana" (p. 4).

Thus, his rejection of this type of narrative discourse is rooted in its concern for extra-literary functions. Its principal goal was social denunciation, and what results was denunciatory at the level of content and therefore flawed as artistic expression.

It is precisely this type of criticism that Benet levels against the widely acclaimed work of one of his best friends: Luis Martin-Santos' *Tiempo de silencio*. Benet's comments on this novel stirred a controversy in Spanish literary circles. One example of the furor is the statement made by Isaac Montero:[21]

> He elegido en general el que me parecía más próximo al usado por Juan Benet en ciertos momentos claves del coloquio y en la casi totalidad de sus intervenciones públicas. Supongo que Benet comprenderá muy bien que mi libertad, en esta opción, ha estado muy mediatizada por el contricante Benet, que ha practicado, *por lo que sé*, todas las arrogancias —incluida la de morder a los muertos, como es el caso de sus declaraciones sobre Luis Martín-Santos— comprenderá mejor que muchos lectores estas servidumbres de las armas (p. 74; italics mine).

Montero justifies the harsh tone of his attack by saying Benet has stooped so low as to insult the dead. But what is most important in the quotation is the phase in italics. It is evident that Montero is unfamiliar with the scope of Benet's comments on the author of *Tiempo de silen-*

21. Whether or not one agrees with Benet's assessment of the trajectory traced by Spanish literature his views bring out several points of particular interest to this study. In the first place one notes the diachronic approach used by the novelist, something that on numerous occasions he argues against in his criticism of literary sociology. Nonetheless his analysis is well-founded on the theoretical framework that he elaborates in his essays. While he does not link the change wrought in Spanish literature to historical events and attitudes, it is nevertheless studied on literary grounds, that is to say, on the basis of the way in which Spain's literary system reacted to changes in historical attitudes, and the effects of these changes on the system. In other words, from the moment that the reaction against the grand style appeared, it continued to be reflected in the course of Spanish literary development from that time on. It is also important to note that the same value system at work earlier is in place here. Literature is once again judged on the basis of its intrinsic merit.

cio. More serious still, is the fact that he has fallen into the trap of confusing a literary judgment on Martín-Santos' work with Benet's personal judgment of the author. Had Montero taken the time to examine more than the sensational elements of Benet's remarks, he would have been able to separate the two aspects he has confused.

Dissatisfaction with *Tiempo de silencio* is, as was mentioned above, founded on bases easily explicable within the parameters of Benet's literary canons. It does not imply a personal dislike for the author. As with his polemical opinions on Galdós, one can reject Benet's views, but that does not change the fact that they agree with his assertions about literature. Although qualitatively superior to other post-war narrative, *Tiempo de silencio* contains the same defects perceptible in most of this period's fiction. When asked his opinion of Martin-Santos in the Núñez interview the author responded in the following manner:

> La pregunta es muy delicada. Quizás el mayor bache que se produjo en nuestra amistad lo originó una opinión bastante descortés y poco atenta sobre *Tiempo de silencio*. Interesó esta novela, pero no me gustó nada. Y no creo que sea una novela de mucho fondo, pero evidentemente ha ejercido y está ejerciendo bastante influencia. Se trata, a mi modo de ver, de una estampa más, aunque aureoleada. ¡Qué sé yo!, por un intento lingüístico considerable y un anhelo y afán por la ironía que a mí me fatigan bastante. Y si es una sátira mejor será decirlo de una vez para siempre. Yo leía el borrador de la segunda novela que dejó poco más a la mitad, con el título de *Tiempo de destrucción* me parece, y creo que se trataba de una novela muy superior a la primera, más seria y menos folletinesca (p. 4).

This passage demonstrates that Benet's opinion of Martín-Santos' novel is guided by the same aesthetic principles that shape his assessment of post-war fiction in general. His comment on its satirical nature alludes to *Tiempo de silencio*'s sociological intent. Given its extraliterary goal, the novel is appraised as lacking in depth, precisely because it becomes so concerned with sociological concerns that it subverts aesthetic ones. Another portion of the quotation points out that the motivation behind Benet's criticism of this novel is literary and not personal as Montero intimated. The praise bestowed on *Tiempo de destrucción* (Barcelona: Seix Barral, 1975) would not have been forthcoming if personal rather than artistic differences had generated Benet's commentary.

Poor quality and extraliterary goals aside, Benet's distaste for post-war narrative fiction is also based on his belief that fiction of this period is dominated by an overbearing concern for *la novelística*.[22] In this respect he chastizes Spanish novelists for their attempts to subsume their creations to a given artistic mold, i.e. social realism, or objectivist fiction. This period's pervasive social tyranny is also denounced. As he states in the "Respuesta a Montero," published in the sames issue *Cuadernos*, pp 75-75.

Un poco más excesiva es su ambición de monopolizar la cultura y el enemigo. Durante años ha servido una cultura tan ramplona como una alpargata, y tan aromática como un insecticida, que cierto buen público se ha visto obligado a tolerar e incluso a aplaudir bajo la coacción de la culpa colectiva, pues de no hacerlo así quedaban alienados juntos a los censores oficiales y las fuerzas del orden. Y cuando ciertamente empieza a sugerir en España algo distinto de aquella sordidez, no pueden hacer menos de inventar una conjura atentoria a la salud de la moza morena (p 76).

Benet's vision of the Spanish post-war novel extracted from the opinions so far examined is not a very positive one but is predicated on an overarching literary value system. Such criticism must not be translated into an overall condemnation of literature that commits itself to

22. La *novelística*, one of the most derogatory terms employed by Benet, is vilified on a number of occasions, especially during his participation in the Mesa Redonda Sobre Novel organized by *Cuadernos para el Diálogo*, and published by that journal in their special number 23 (December 1970), pp. 45-52.

social commentary. It is a rather an attack on that literature which, by so doing, fails on a literary level. The author's opinions expressed in the *encuesta* on social literature contained in Eduardo García Rico's *Literatura y política. En torno al realismo español* (Madrid: Cuadernos para el Diálogo, 1971) support my contention and must be studied carefully.

Para quien no está obligado por su oficio a conocer toda la producción de una determinada rama de la cultura, tarde o temprano aquellos artículos que se conforman con su gusto se van imponiendo a aquellos que gozan de menor predilección. De esa suerte, el gusto —formado a partir de una selección de los conocimientos primeros— se convierte en una determinante principal del conocimiento, que acostumbra a progresar en cuanto aquel, no estando saturado, puede presentar una vía abierta a la incitación. Me resulta incómodo opinar sobre una corriente literaria que, por aparejarme mal a mi gusto, sólo conocí muy superficialmente: quiero suponer que su mejor justificación está en el hecho de que en aquellos años apenas se podía hacer otra cosa. La situación cultural se hallaba dominada totalmente por la política, de suerte que el más tímido intento de independizar la cultura de la política había de empezar por las zonas fronterizas entre ambas, esto es —y por decirlo así— las zonas propiamente menos cultas de la cultura. Así, pues, para buscar la independencia de juicio y de gusto era menester pasar a la oposición tanto de la literatura patriótica como de la neutra —fuera blanca, rosa o de acentuado color local—, para la cual el cúmulo de inquietud, arbitrariamente e injusticia de la vida social ofrecía un campo inagotable. La desgracia de esa literatura fiscal es que ni siquiera podía hablar de la tragedia en toda su extensión; estaba casi amordazada, y lo que se leía en las novelas de la acusación era un pálido remedo de lo que pasaba en el país. En cuanto a la información, suministraba mucho menos que lo que el hombre despierto podía recoger en la calle, y en cuanto a estilo, había hecho renuncia voluntaria de toda dificultad en gracia de la severidad y la sequedad de las sentencias. Y si bien me parece de poca utilidad establecer el balance cultural ateniéndose a cánones que entonces no eran posibles, es forzoso reconocer que el esfuerzo de aquellos hombres que alzaron su protesta colaboró a una mayor independencia de la cultura y fue el acicate para una reacción que para ser duradera ha de haberse en algo más que la oposición a la primera tendencia (p. 19).

The measured tone of this statement contrasts with that of Benet's other pronouncements on contemporary Spanish narrative. He refrains from controversial statements and expresses in a clear and succinct manner his opinions of a type of literature that is out of tune with his aesthetic principles. Aside from this difference in tone, the commentary is important for two reasons: the way in which it modifies his other comments on the subject, and the insights that it provides on his view of francoist Spain, a subject that will be examined in detail below.

Opinions on the post-war novel given in the *encuesta* add a dimension not found in Benet's earlier comments. Until this juncture his remarks on socially oriented literature had centered on its literary inefficiency.[23] Here a stance on the moral commitment manifested in this type of literature is added. His tacit approval of the endeavors of the so-called *escritores fiscales* (committed writers of his generation) demonstrates this. While disapproving of both their artistic credo and the resultant literary works, he admits that it was the only response possible on both ethical and literary levels in an unacceptable socio-cultural ambience. Novelists attempted to breathe life into Spanish literature and, simultaneously, to open the cultural milieu that was controlled by francoist ideological precepts, and dominated by escapist and triumphalist literature. At the same time they protested

23. None of the author's recent public pronouncement or articles on the subject alter this view. See "Una época troyana," in *En ciernes* (Madrid: Taurus, 1976), and "La novela en la España de hoy (1980)," in *La moviola de Eurípides* (Madrid: Taurus, 1981), and Benet's participation in the Ciclo de Novela Española Contemporánea held at the Fundación Juan March (2-7 June 1975). These remarks were later published in the *Novela Española Actual* (Madrid: Fundación Juan March/ Editorial Cátedra, 1977).

against, and tried to change, the socio-political situation that was responsible for Spain's arid cultural atmosphere. Such endeavors were both literarily and politically inefficacious. Due to the restrictions of censorship they could provide only the *pálido remedo* of what was directly ascertainable on the street. Though doomed to both artisic and political failure, the attempts of his contemporaries did serve, Benet admits, to rejuvenate Spain's cultural atmosphere, and in some ways redirect the country's literary trajectory by removing Spanish literature from the exclusive control of those who supported the regime's ideology.

What is added to previous statements in the García Rico book, then, shows that Benet's disapproval of the post-war novel and socially oriented literature in general is not motivated by an *a priori* rejection of this type of literature. His support of the moral and ethical motivations of the writers of the Generación de Medio Siglo indicates that he disapproves of the *way* socially committed writers go about their task, not of the fact that the task in undertaken. This clarification is crucial to an accurate assessment of the writer's view of this type of literary act, for it aligns him with many other writers of his era who, in retrospect, voiced similar opinions about novelistic production: that socially committed ideas must be couched in an aesthetic artifact capable of enduring on its own artistic merits.

Conclusions:

Juan Benet and Anti-francoist Ideology

Statements on francoist Spain, indirectly introduced in the discussion of Benet's literary views, augur poorly for any attempt to characterize him as a reactionary. A systematic review of his comments on the subject supports my assertions that he fits within the boundaries of the anti-regime collective subject. The impact of the Spanish Civil War on his personal life, explained in the Núñez interview, is extended to the conflict's national consequences in the Tola de Habich comments.

65

Si hablamos de los últimos treinta años, por ejemplo, que es un plazo bastante amplio, o de la guerra civil, realmente no es que haya una decadencia de la literatura española, sino una decadencia de la vida española completa, que se refleja en el pensamiento, en la política, en la ciencia, en la calle, en la arquitectura... y en las mujeres, si me insisten: Parece que en las mujeres menos. Pero no sé de ninguna manifestación de la vida española que no sea expresión de una decadencia. Y no sólo espiritual, sino moral, física (p. 39).

The decadence he perceives in post-war Spain dates from the Civil War, whose outcome served to initiate a corroding process touching all aspects of Spanish life. The Tola de Habich interview also demonstrates Benet's pessimism about Spain under Franco, something explored in greater detail in the Campbell interview.[24]

Other manifestations of his disapproval with the regime and its supporters are presented early in the Baroja piece cited above. When speaking about the closing of France's border with Spain as a result of the 1946 United Nations resolutions condemning the Spanish government, Benet comments on how reactions to the isolation in which this move placed Spain differed according to one's political outlook.

Quiero decir, a todos los que habíamos sido educados en un clima liberal y esperábamos de cada día que se produjera el fin de una cierta situación. Porque otros que probablemente eran los más, en un amplio sector de la sociedad madrileña, parecían hallarse en aquel ambiente de renovada jactancia y patriotismo de campanario, como peces en el agua; y hasta los modales oficiales y públicos del país se volvieron más agresivos que en los últimos años de la Guerra Mundial, cuando el desarrollo de los acontecimientos militares vino a poner cierto freno a algunas actitudes excesivamente nacionalistas para sustituirlas por esa ambigüedad de conducta que constituía la mejor postura ante una historia que nadie sabía hacia

24. See especially p. 299.

dónde iba a dirigirse. Pero con el cierre de la frontera se acabó la tregua o, mejor dicho, la suspensión de cierto grado de tolerancia. Las pocas personas que discrepaban de la ideología oficial se encontraban en la calle como conspiradores que habrían hecho las delicias de Alejandro Dumas; se refugiaban en un portal a cambiar unos comentarios y, cuando más, buscaban un café desierto, una ala solitaria y una mesa aislada, para hablar muy bajo (pp. 11-12).

One senses in this excerpt Benet's uneasiness in the period's hostile environment, and his disagreement with the political structure whose policies were responsible for it. The regime is characterized by the repressive manner in which it dealt with those disagreeing with its official ideology, here manifested in the way it ostracized as "conspiradores" all who deviated from officially espoused political positions. It is important to note that Benet identifies with this minority of Spaniards desirous of a change in the status quo ("el fin de una cierta situación") which was diametrically opposed to the "clima liberal" that characterized the pre-war period of his childhood. By identifying with this minority, he separates both himself and those who shared his wish from "los más" who were comfortable in the atmosphere of "jactancia y patriotismo de campanario" characteristic of the era.[25]

Other sections of the Baroja piece underscore the writers's disagreement with the francoist regime, expanding on the political differences sketched above, to demonstrate the psychological impact that living in a society where the possibility of a much desired change towards a more democratic social structure was totally absent could axercisa on an individual.[26]

---

25. Barbara Probst Solomon's book (see n. 1) contains interesting information on the Benet family, especially on Juan's brother Paco, an ardent opponen of the francoist regime who had a profound impact on his brother.

26. Más que difícil, resulta insoportable una vida que no se deja amenizar por la seducción de la noticia subversiva, por la inminencia del acontecimiento que todo lo ha de transformar. La realidad cotidiana entre 1945-1955 ofrecía tan escasos motivos de estímulo y entusiasmo, que se comprende, sin necesidad de recurrir a las simplificaciones del psicoanálisis, la afición a buscar una cierta amenidad en una zona

Two recent statements by the author which thus far have elicited scant critical comment are imperative to a correct assessment of the Civil War's role in mediating life in post-war Spain. An examination of them shows how Benet fits within the ideological parameters of the anti-regime world view.

In remarks made at the Ciclo de Novela Española Contemporánea held in July 1975, at the Fundación March in Madrid, and reported in that institution's *Hoja Informativa de Literatura y Filología* (July, 1975, p. 4), Benet made the following important comment on the war's impact on his country. "En la historia española la verdadera guerra que cambió y marcará para siempre al país ha sido la última. Esto es lo que he pretendido decir con mis novelas."[27] This statement is noteworthy both because of its directness and the way it establishes a tangible link between the novelist's social views and his fiction. In *¿Qué fue la guerra civil?* (Barcelona: La Gaya Ciencia, 1976), an important monograph that appeared only a year after his remarks at the Fundación March, significant amplifications are perceptible in his views. For this study, the pamphlet's first section, "La sombra de la guerra civil," is crucial. In its first paragraph the writer makes the following assertions as to the Civil War's deleterious effects:

La Guerra Civil de 1936 a 1939 fue, sin duda alguna, el acontecimiento histórico más importante de la España contemporánea y quién sabe si el más decisivo de su historia. Nada ha conformado de tal manera la vida de los españoles del Siglo XX y todavía está lejos el día en que los hombres de esta tierra se pueden sentir libres del peso y la sombra que arroja todavía aquel funesto conflicto. Exac-

escatológica de la fantasía que está más cerca del portento que de la casualidad. Pero el mentis diario, que el curso rutinario de los acontecimientos impone a unas esperanzas mal concebidas, a menudo da origen a un escepticismo de segundo grado, una suerte de perverso regocijo en la adversidad y un desquiciamiento de la credulidad, porque a medida que lo esperado se torna improbable, más deseable se hace lo inverosímil (pp. 19-20).

27. The remarks reported in the *Boletín Informativo* were later published in *Novela española actual* (see n. 23).

tamente cuarenta años y una quincena después del día en que se
inició ha sido necesario un perdón real para borrar —parcial y jurí-
dicamente— las heridas aún abiertas y profundas divisiones que
desde aquella lejana fecha, al seguir separando al país en campos
difícilmente conciliables, preservan de un estado latente, cuando
no abierta belicosidad (p. 9).

While the rest of Europe left its war behind to rebuild from the ruins,
Spain has not done so, especially in the ideological/political sphere.
The denunciation of the repressive and retarding effects that the war's
outcome and the institutionalization of the francoist regime had on
post-war Spain finds its most lucid expression in the following passage.
Here the author's view of francoism's corrosive effects in obstructing
normal socio-cultural development and maintaining an ambience
based on the ideological schism that precipitated the Civil War is made
clear.

En contraste con Europa, España durante cuarenta años ha vivido
—oficialmente— glorificando la guerra, manteniendo elevada la
guardia, usufructando las rentas de la victoria y pretendiendo hacer
de semejante estado un régimen estable y definitivo para todo el
pueblo español. ¿Se imagina alguien a alemanes, italianos, austría-
cos, croatas o japoneses tratados en 1976 por sus vecinos y antiguos
enemigos como lo han sido los republicanos españoles hasta el día
de hoy? El desarrollo de los últimos treinta años ¿hubiera sido posi-
ble con tal política? Afortunadamente nadie será capaz de medir lo
que semejante tratamiento ha supuesto para el progreso y la evolu-
ción de la sociedad española pero aquellos que se han atribuido la
paternidad de ese desarrollo y han llegado a dar su apellido a la paz
de la posguerra serán en su día justamente inculpados por la historia como los mayores retardarios de nuestro progreso y los más cali-
ficados agentes contraceptivos de la regeneración que necesita el
país (pp. 10-11).[28]

28. Humor normally manifested in the form of sarcasm is also used to convey Benet's

The line of argumentation pursued in the last several pages has as its goal a re-evaluation of two closely linked elements: Benet's position with reference to the post-war Spanish novel and his view of francoist Spain. This reassessment serves a useful purpose for several reasons. The evidence examined indicates that there is in Benet a perceptible manifestation of ideas conducive to the postulation of an anti-regime ideology underlying the narrative surface-message of *Volverás a Región*. It also points out the novelist's support for the narrative projects of writers of his generation, even when he is not completely satisfied with the artistic elaboration of those projects. What emerges from the analysis undertaken above is a view of Benet's opinions that differs substantially from what other critics have said about his world view and the social scope of his narrative.

Hence, a careful scrutiny of his statements on Spain and its literature rectifies the image of a detached elitist, and replaces it with one of an author who articulates social views similar in structure (although not always in content) to those espoused by writers normally thought to be more socially progressive.

It is at this juncture that a link necdoro be established between social views and literary values, between essayistic and narrative praxis. I have consistently emphasized that Benet's criticism of the socially oriented literature of his generation is based on his unwillingness to accept a literary work that is not first of all of artistic merit, but that does not preclude the possibility of literature's fulfilling a socially critical function. Hinted at in the García Rico piece, this is the attitude that Benet brings to his own fiction; works which articulate at a literary level the unarticulated element of his essays: the confluence of literary excellence and socially critical intent.

---

disapproval with the socio-political situation as it existed in the Spain of that period. This is normally accomplished through the insertion of caustic comments about the regime and its policies. See especially the "Barojiana" essay and his answers to the *Encuesta* on literature and education in Spain in *Literatura y educación*, ed. Fernando Lázaro Carreter (Madrid: Castalia 1974), pp. 197-206.

CHAPTER III

Volverás a Región

Structure and World View

I

Analysis of *Histoire*

Criticis who have dealt with the action that takes place in *Volverás a Región* have emphasized that it lacks what is traditionally conceived of as plot. In formulating such appraisals they look for other methods to categorize the novel's action. Such an approach can be found in David K. Herzberger's excellent study *The Novelistic World of Juan Benet* (Clear Creek, Indiana: The American Hispanist, 1977). "What has traditionally been called the 'plot' of a novel does not exist in *Volverás a Región*. Instead, the novel consists of a complex framework of third-person narration and pseudo-dialogues between the two principal characters, Dr. Sebastián and Gamallo's daughter" (p. 43). Almost identical sentiments are voiced in Vicente Cabrera's unpublishhed paper "*Volverás a Región*: An Antithetical Pattern of Enigma." "Juan Benet's first novel *Volverás a Región* (1967) has, instead of a readily traceable plot in the traditional sense, two integrating and integrated situations which are briefly mentioned at the beginning of the novel, laconically developed throughout and never clearly revealed in their entirety." Up to a certain point, I agree with these assertions. One could not, for example, compare the plot structure of Benet's work to traditional examples of such highly plotted fiction as the nineteenth-century realist novel. On the other hand, if such standards are applied generally to modern narratives there will obviously be a significant degree of deviance from the realist norm. In addition, the very concept of plot itself can be employed ambiguously.

73

Volverás a Región might easily be compared to Carpentier's *El acoso*, Rulfo's *Pedro Páramo*, or other representative examples of highly complex modern Hispanic fiction.[1] In all, a fragmented narrative syntax scatters the component elements of the *histoire* throughout the *discours*, posing formidable difficulties for the reader attempting to reconstruct the order of events. While critics have dealt efficiently with the structural complexities posed by its Latin American counterparts, such is not the case with Benet's first novel. Part of the problem resides in the author's newness as an object of critical assessments. The bibliography surrounding his work grows astoundingly each year, but much of what is produced is still of a descriptive nature, with few studies closely analyzing specific aspects of his narratives.

Although the aforementioned factors contribute to the problem, its crux lies elsewhere. The ambiguity inherent in such traditional terminology as plot, and the fuzziness with which that term is sometimes applied, are the main culprits in the failure to delineate accurately the action occurring in *Volverás a Región*. The idea of plot as it is used in most critical assessments stems from Aristotle's *Poetics*. An explanation which highlights the essential elements of the Aristotelian definition can be found in the glossary of a widely used critical primer: *A Handbook of Critical Approaches to Literature*, ed. Wilfred L. Guerin *et al.* (New York: Harper and Row, 1966), where it is characterized as "The action, that which happens —narratively speaking— in a literary work. Technically, it involves not only a sequence of episodes but their interaction and interrelation in a dynamic structure" (p. 228).

The Princeton Encyclopedia of Poetry and Poetics, ed. Alex Preminger *et. al.* (Princeton, New Jersey: Princeton University Press, 1966), however, points out that from time to time in the history of criticism, the concept of plot has shifted, as critics have stressed either the making of the work or the response to it. "Viewed in terms of the prin-

---

1. An interesting study dealing with the parallels between Rulfo's and Benet's novels is Esther Nelson's unpublished essay "The Aesthetics of Refraction: A Comparative Study of *Pedro Páramo* and *Volverás a Región*.

ciples controling the making of a work of art, plot has referred to action, to pattern, to structure, or to some variation of these elements; viewed in terms of the psychological and emotional response of the audience or reader, plot has referred to impressionism, to sense of unity, to purpose, or to some similar response" (p. 623). Thus behind the deceptive simplicity of the first definition cited, lies the inherent multiplicity of ways in which terminology can be and has been applied.

Such a profusion of definitions can lead to problems of ambiguity, and it is just this type of critical ambivalence which hinders a correct assessment of the action in *Volverás a Región*. Both Herzberger and Cabrera, for instance, maintain that Benet's novel lacks a plot in the "traditional" sense. But "traditional" can mean many different things. Moreover, the types of alternatives that are suggested to characterize the novel's action make one suspect they are using this term in two different ways.

It is precisely the wish to avoid such problems that has led to the employment of the structuralist dichotomy between *histoire* and *discours*. By separating them, the critic is able to avoid many difficulties. While *Volverás a Región* may not have a well-developed plot line, it does present an accessibly segmentable *histoire*, albeit one whose components are scattered throughout the *discours*. The failure of traditional methodology to differentiate between these two elements is at least partially responsible for the inability of the critical appraisals cited above to come to grips with action and its syntactical dispositon in Benet's text. The alternatives offered by the two critics would, in fact, both fall under the heading of *discours*, as they clearly are concerned with the action's disposition in the novel. Thus, rather than finding an alternative to plot to categorize the action, they have only described another aspect of it: the manner in which it is incorporated into the work's narrative syntax.

The first step in any attempt to fix the novel's *histoire* entails arriving ar a workable paraphase of its actions from which its main sequences can be abstracted. This paraphrase will recast the narrative line of the text in chronological order, and must account for as many of the action's important elements as possible.[2]

The major characters involved here are: Gamallo, a military officer; María Timoner, his lover or fiancée; Dr. Daniel Sebastián; an unnamed card player; Marré Gamallo, the officer's daughter;[3] Luis I. Timoner, María's son; and a boy whose mother was forced to leave him during the war. These are, of course, not all the characters who appear in the novel. But they are the ones whose roles are most important to the central narrative elaborated in the text.

My paraphrase of the action in *Volverás a Región* is as follows. Gamallo is a young military officer, reared by his aunts in an abnormal home situation. This upbringing has seemingly scarred him for life, and has inculcated him with somewhat perverted values. One night, in Región's casino, he begins a card game with an unnamed opponent. The latter has in his possession a strange gold coin given to him by a mysterious woman. As the card sessions progress, Gamallo's desire to obtain the coin evinces noticeable changes in his comportment. This situation causes a rift between him and his fiancée/lover, María Timoner, who is staying under the care of Dr. Sebastián, in a local sanatorium, because of Gamallo's fears that public opinion would frown on their relationship. Dr. Sebastián, whose upbringing is strikingly parallel to Gamallo's, begins to fall in love with María as a result of the time he spends with her. She, in turn, is growing fearful of the changes the card game is producing in her lover. Gamallo now pays almost no

2. Several essays on Benet's first novel provide information on its action which can help in this process. They include four previously mentioned studies: Gimferrer's *Plural* article, Herzberger's monograph, José Ortega's article, and Gonzalo Sobejano's book. Also useful is Alberto Oliart's "Viaje a Región," *Revista de Occidente,* NS 80 (November 1969), pp. 224-234. In the course of a radically different reading of the novel than is presented in this essay, Luis Costa's "El lector-viajero en *Volverás a Región,*" *Anales de la Narrativa Española Contemporánea,* 4 (1979), 9-19, presents information of a useful nature regarding the novel's action sequences.

3. Many critics refer to this character only as Gamallo's daughter. Her first name appears only once in the narrative (p. 115). Two critics were the first to point this out: Esther Nelson in "Narrative Perspective in *Volverás a Región, The American Hispanist,* 4, No. 36 (May 1979), 3-6; and Teresa Aveleyra in "Algo sobre las criaturas de Juan Benet," *Nueva Revista de Filología Hispánica,* 23 (1974), 121-130.

attention to her, so intense is his concentration on his objective: winning the gold coin. When all other stakes are exhausted he bets María's engagement ring, and, by extension, María herself. The doctor, taking advantage of Maria's waning interest in the officer (and the latter's total absorption in the game) makes plans to flee with her. His plans are thwarted, however, when the unknown card player finally wins the ring, and María, and both flee to the mountains, after the card player maims Gamallo by stabbing him in the hand. The officer and his friends persue them on horseback, but their efforts are futile. Both the doctor and Gamallo are marked for life (physically and emotionally) by their respective losses.

María subsequently summons the doctor to her side to deliver her son by the card player. She names the child Luis I. Timoner, and the doctor becomes his godfather. Sebastián makes periodic trips to her out-of-the-way refuge in Mantua to care for her (she is now suffering from some type of venereal disease) and the boy. María later dies from the effects of the disease, which have left her so disfigured that she constantly wears a veil.

The Civil War breaks out. Gamallo's military career has been in a state of limbo following his disgrace in the card game. Although eminently unqualified, he becomes, almost by chance, the Nationalist officer in charge of the conquest of Región. He enjoys the task, since it affords him the opportunity to gain a measure of revenge that he was unable to achieve years before. His handling of the campaign proves successful, and he wins a series of promotions until he finally attains the rank of general.

His daughter, Marré, is being raised in Región away from her father in a home situation analogous to the one he experienced as a child. During the war Región's Republican defenders attempt to use her as a hostage to bargain with her father. Gamallo, however, refuses to accede to their demands. In the waning days of the military action, the impending arrival of the Nationalist troops causes many of Región's defenders to flee, and they take Marré with them. There, in the mountains, she meets Luis I. Timoner, who has fled from his mother, and

77

with him experiences the only meaningful relationship of her life. With the capture of Región near; Gamallo is killed, and thus for a second time fails to gain his revenge. Región is captured, and Marré is liberated by its conquerers. Luis flees, and is never heard of again. Marré is brought back and "rehabilitated," but she is unable to endure life after the changes she has undergone as a result of her war-time experiences, most especially her contact with Luis.

Years later, she finally escapes and once again returns to Región in an attempt to find Luis and to recapture the ephemeral happiness she knew. On her journey she calls on Dr. Sebastián in the hope he will have some information that can guide her in this search. They carry on a long conversation in which important moments of their lives are brought out.

The doctor has been living in a state of almost suspended animation, most of his time being dedicated to drinking. His sanatorium now has only one patient. This is a half-crazed young man, whose mother was forced to leave him a child during the war, never to return. Her failure to do so is responsible for his condition. When he sees Marré approach in the same type of black car in which his mother "abandoned" him years ago, he becomes excited in the expectation that she has finally returned. His excitement turns to rage when Marré departs to continue her journey. As the text closes, his rage precipitates his killing of Daniel Sebastián. The action ends soon afterward with the sound of a distant carbine, signalling Marré's death at the hands of the mysterious Numa.

The above description of the action reveals several facts. The first is that the majority of the characters involved are closely bound by a web of interpersonal relationships, as Schematic I clearly demonstrates. In addition, the *histoire*'s constituent actions begin as a result of the card game and the events that directly ensue from it. This has led Oliart to conceive of María Timoner as the novel's most important personage, since she causes its action to congeal. "Si pudiera hablarse de un personaje central en la novela, éste sería María Timoner. Alrededor de María Timoner por razones amorosas o filiales, están el Doc-

SCHEMATIC I
Volverás a Región
Character Interrelationships

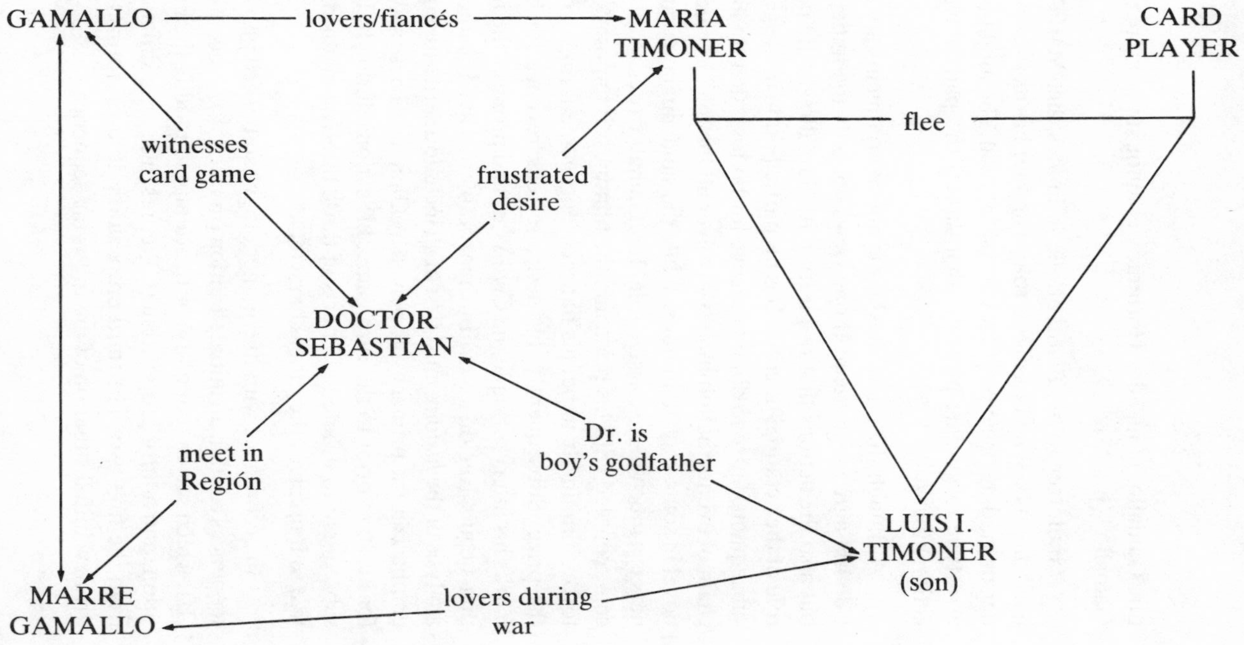

CARD
PLAYER

flee

MARIA
TIMONER

LUIS I.
TIMONER
(son)

GAMALLO

lovers/fiancés

frustrated
desire

Dr. is
boy's godfather

lovers during
war

witnesses
card game

DOCTOR
SEBASTIAN

meet in
Región

MARRE
GAMALLO

79

tor, Gamallo, el jugador Hortera, y el amor sin nombre de la hija de Gamallo" (p. 225).[4]

Gimferrer in his *Plural* article intimates that María's last name itself might be symbolic of this role. Timoner has its root in *timón* (rudder or guiding principle). By extensión, then, she might be perceived as a type of guiding principle that directs the path along which the action moves.

Although the main lines of the above arguments are reasonable, I do not agree with them. If one views not only the initial card game, but also the actions that result from it, Gamallo should be cast in the role of the actantial fulcrum. It is his participation in the game, and his subsequent desire to obtain revenge for his loss, that set in motion the chain of events that ultimately involves all the major characters of the novel in some way or another. While the same might be said of María, hers is a much more passive role. It is Gamallo's desire to win the gold coin, coupled with his pride and the blindness it imposes on him, that forces him finally to bet his fiancée's engagement ring in order to win the prize. Subsequently, his desire to seek revenge for his maiming marks his intervention in the Civil War, and prompts the final process that begins Región's slow but inexorable decay. For these reasons, analysis of the *histoire* must first of all include a series of sequences that emphasizes the primary role played by Gamallo. These should account for his state prior to the card game, his actions during it, his behavior subsequent to it, and the effects of those three elements on the narrative as it involves the other characters.

In accordance with the methodology established previously these sequences contain an initial situation (marked A), a second propositon (B), which serves to modify, or to attempt to modify the initial proposition, and a third proposition (C) representing the situation resulting from the first two. The third proposition, in turn, forms the basis for the new initial situation of the following sequence.

---

4. Oliart fails to perceive that Marré's "amor sin nombre" does in fact have a name: Luis I. Timoner.

As shown in the schematic, each of the initial propositions of the Gamallo series involves some type of frustration on his part. In IA, it is the result of a strange family background that has inculcated him with an equally strange set of values.[5] It is this value system that is essentially responsible for the ultimate alienation of María. Gamallo's wish to maintain appearances, for example, motivates him to keep her virtually incarcerated as a patient in the sanatorium.[6] In addition, his

5. This is clearly indicated in the text. Gamallo's rearing by his aunts, in the absence of his father, profoundly shapes the views of the child described in the following passage:
...caían sin resuello en los viejos sillones de mimbre para concentrar sobre el niño una unánime mirada de la que se destilaba todo el encono, la esperanza diferida y el recelo de una condición que no se decidía a unirse al hombre por el temor a perder su dinero; he ahí el rayo que en la mente del niño fijará para siempre en el negativo horrendo —un corro de mudas y adormitorias miradas en el fondo de la penumbre veraniega, con el zumbido de los abanicos y el agitado aliento de los pechos enlutados—, el signo indeleble de su propia formación: volverá a relevarlo, años más tarde en los momentos de combate; ante la mesa de juego, al abalanzarse sobre un montón de fichas de nácar, ajeno, siempre ajeno, al gesto de una mujer que retrocede por los salones vacíos mientras el público corre hacia la mesa donde su mano quedó atravesada por la navaja; a lomos de la mula holgazana, la mente (espoleada por el eco vengativo y rencoroso de los abanicos) preocupada tan sólo por el peso de la moneda que nunca llegó a tener en la mano. Porque todo esto estaba previsto y decidido como consecuencia de una formación que descansaba sobre este sobreentendido; tal era el deber —a la sazón su padre había descendido ya el reino de la sombras; nunca le había escrito y sólo de tarde en tarde, entre sueños, asomaba la melancolía de una expresión, envuelta en una luz cerúlea que apenas iluminaba el pómulo y la frente taciturna, en la que no había censura sino una mitigada pero insalvable retracción nacida de un concepto diferente del dinero—, un correlato de la gloria del apellido, un dogma para revestir de recelo el objeto de su afán, una forma hereditaria de defensa ante las imposturas del alma (pp. 70-71). All quotations from the novel are taken from the first edition (Barcelona: Ediciones Destino, 1967).
    It is interesting to note that many of the major characters described in the *histoire* suffered through what might be called an "abnormal" childhood. In "Prohibition and Transgression in Two Novels of Juan Benet," *The American Hispanist*, 4 No. 36 (May 1979), 20-24, Stephen Summerhill points out that "...the author gives considerable emphasis to the childhood of the characters, particularly the restrictive and combining aspect of their upbringing" (p. 22).

6. No se le había ocultado a él, desde los primeros días, que se trataba de su amante quien además de inducirla a trasladarse allí para tenerla cerca e iniciar su incorporación a la sociedad regionata no quería de ninguna manera verse envuelto —gracia de la reputación de su nombre, de la posición que gozaban sus tías, y de la herencia que de ellas esperaba— en un tipo de relación que se traducía en escándalo, pondría en compromiso aquellas prendas o le abocaría irremediablemente el matrimonio. Para un caso tal la clínica ofrecía una solución y un refugio (pp. 234-235).

pride and fixation on the game cause him to ignore her almost completely and, ultimately, to make her the contest's final stake.

The resultant frustration in IC implies much more than the psychological scars of chilhood and adolescence. Gamallo's maiming at the hands of the card player, and the disappointment of both losing María and not obtaining the coin, coupled with the disgrace implicit in them, will shape the rest of his life. They precipitate his revengeful pursuit of María and the stranger. This action also results in the frustration seen in proposition IIC. Unable to obtain revenge, Gamallo is in essentially the same position that characterized him in IC. His maiming and frustration also halt, for all intents and purposes, his military career, and paralyze his personal life. Years later, they inspire a second quest for revenge, this time through participation in the Civil War. Both attempts are, of course, crucial to the text's action. In terms of the *histoire*'s outcome, however, the second bears on it most directly. Here, while the motivation for Gamallo's behavior remains personal, its boundaries are expanded. Rather than an attempt to "punish" several individuals, Gamallo's action is now an attack against Región in general. Having suffered his initial disgrace there, he is now afforded an excellent and unexpected pretext to undertake "punitive" measures against the entire area.

As commander-in-chief of the Nationalist effort to reduce Región, a center of opposition, he is able to masquerade personal vendetta behind the facade of military objective. If his comportment in the past ranged from strange to abnormal, here it might be characterized as reprobate, for he has no strong commitment to the Nationalist cause other than using it as a pretext. In effect, the architect of the Nationalist victory is portrayed as a mentally and physically maimed figure obsessed with the memories surrounding the infliction of his wounds, and with the way to avenge them.

This vital connection between personality and historical action is stressed by Ricardo Gullón in his important study "Una región laberíntica que bien pudiera llamarse España" (*Insula*, No. 319 [June 1973], pp. 3, 10). In this article Gullón also stresses that the card game and the war-time attempt at revenge are closely linked.

El episodio guerrero está ligado al episodio ficticio por una sinécdoque; una mano agarrotada representa al hombre que en 1937 dirige la ofensiva franquista contra Región y sus contornos; el mismo hombre que remontando el curso de la acción jugará una prolongada partida de naipes, clave de la novela, pero clave sólo descifrable muy adelantada la lectura. El episodio guerrero es la jugada final de esa partida, interrumpida veinte años atrás por una navaja que clavó a la mesa la mano de quien se creyó o se fingió ganacioso en el juego.

El lector debe retener en la memoria los datos que le explicarán la pasión del general Gamallo, cuando llegue a saber que la mano deforme no solamente distingue al militar: la representa. Basta mencionar la mano para hacerle presente; por el identificamos al hombre como el mismo que, siendo teniente, en un impreciso ayer, arriesgó fortuna y honor en la empresa de ganar en el juego a quien poesía la moneda de la hechicera, el talismán que aseguraba el triunfo. Para obtener el talismán que le haría invencible, no vaciló en jugar cuando tenía, incluso su amante (p. 1).[7]

While Gamallo's personal attempt at revenge is once again thwarted, as he dies before his troops conquer their objective, its effects on the *comarca* and its inhabitants are monumental. Región is reduced to an area awaiting its ultimate destruction. The characters suffer the same fate. Their futures become nothing more than a continual reminiscence of the past.

Thus, the Gamallo sequence is characterized by several constants. The first is Gamallo's psychological state, itself responsible for the second constant: his repeated attempts to inflict revenge on those whom he deems culpable for his personal losses. As has been seen, these two elements combine in a kind of spiral relationship. Frustra-

---

7. Very similar opinions are expressed by Aveleyra and Ortega. The latter states that: La ruina en Región se identificaba, en la parábola *Volverás a Región* con la del militar Gamallo..." (p. 235). Aveleyra also points out how the game fundamentally changes Gamallo's life. See especially p. 129 of her study.

Schematic II
Gamallo Series
of
Sequences

I.

(A)

Gamallo has abnormal values; Gamallo and María Timoner are lovers/fiancés

(B)

Gamallo engages in card game and bets María to win coin

(C)

Gamallo loses both María and coin, and is maimed and frustrated

II.

(A)

Gamallo is maimed and frustrated

(B)

Gamallo seeks revenge

(C)

Gamallo is frustrated

III.

(A)

Gamallo is maimed and frustrated

(B)

Gamallo seeks revenge as Nationalist soldier

(C)

Gamallo's revenge is frustrated and he is killed

tion results in action to relieve it, which, in turn, only intensifies rather than solves the problem expounded in the sequence's initial situation.

The remainder of the actions described in the paraphrase can be accounted for as a series of sequences that are keyed to the three involving Gamallo. They represent, in effect, sub-series mediated by the actions of the dominant Gamallo string. In each, the life of one of the characters mentioned in the paraphrase is carried forward from the point he is introduced into the master series, or from the juncture that his life becomes related to it. Exceptions to this are the card player and the disturbed child. The former's fate is never mentioned after the chase. The child, while not directly related to the events of the Gamallo series, is indirectly joined to it through the effects generated by its third sequence.

A series of sequences can be written for each of the other characters discussed in the paraphrase (María, Dr. Sebastián, Marré Gamallo, Luis I. Timoner, and the disturbed patient in the doctor's sanatorium) in which each of them serves as the protagonist. I must emphasize, however, that insofar as their actions are mediated by the Gamallo series, they are, in effect, actantially secondary to the dominant role he plays in the structure of the novel's *histoire*.

As Schematic III shows, I have also transcribed that portion of the *histoire* dealing with María Timoner as three sequences. They too highlight the importance that the card game has as a determining factor on the subsequent events of her life, for as a result of it, her life takes on the character of a one-directional flow. From abandonment by the card player, isolation, and the maiming effects of her disease, an inexorable path is charted that ultimately leads to her death. The structure of the *histoire* amply bears this out. Both the actions undertaken in IB and IIIB, as well as the effect of the card player's flight in IIB, have the same qualitative effect seen in the initial and final propositions of the sequences: they all lead to some type of physical or mental isolation, or state of abandonment. Hence, the nascent alienation and solitude presented in the initial proposition (IA) is continually intensified throughout the three sequences.

Like the vain officer who makes her its stakes, the card game and its results cause María the same type of mental and physical maiming that is inflicted on him. Just as was the case with the relationship between the soldier's defeat and his quest for revenge, the two maiming processes at work in María are also interrelated. On the psychological level, the game causes the initial alienation from her lover, which ultimately results in her abandonment of him in favor of other alternatives. But the game is also responsible for her physical disfigurement, the end result of her sexual contact with the card player. This physical state, in turn, serves to feed the psychological one. The former makes her want to hide herself so that nobody can see her. This in itself, thus, accounts for her physical isolation from others.

In terms of the structure of the *histoire*, therefore, Gamallo's actions must be construed as directly responsible for María's condition. His abnormal character and behavior leads to his treating her in a way that alienates her. She is totally subjugated to his desire first to win the gold coin, and then to achieve revenge. In a strange and passive way, she is both the object and cause of his attempts to destroy the *comarca* of Región.

The segment of the *histoire* dealing directly with the doctor has also been transcribed as three sequences (see Schematic IV). In addition to this superficial one, there are a variety of more important similarities between this series and the previous two. Doctor Daniel Sebastián's family upbringing evinces marked similarities with Gamallo's. Particularly interesting are the parallel roles played by females in shaping both their childhood and adolescence.[8] This home ambience accounts for the frustration manifested in the initial proposition of the series (IA). In effect, this state continually intensifies throughtout the three sequences. Attempts to reduce or mediate it by means of the actions in propositions IB and IIB are unsuccessful, and they result in no substantial alteration of the doctor's condition, as can be seen in propositions IC and IIC.

8. The quotation dealing with Gamallo's childhood (see n. 5) and the description of Daniel Sebastián's youth (pp. 120-122) underscore this similarity.

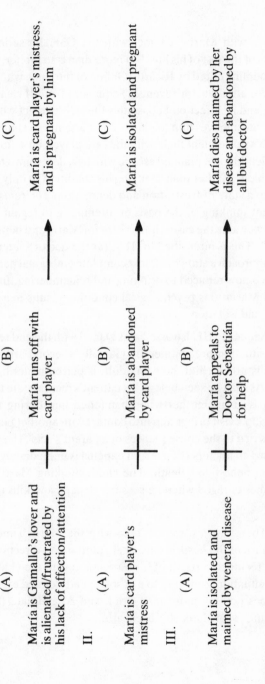

**Schematic III
María Timoner
Series of
Sequences**

I.

(A)

María is Gamallo's lover and is alienated/frustrated by his lack of affection/attention

(B)

María runs off with card player

(C)

María is card player's mistress, and is pregnant by him

II.

(A)

María is card player's mistress

(B)

María is abandoned by card player

(C)

María is isolated and pregnant

III.

(A)

María is isolated and maimed by veneral disease

(B)

María appeals to Doctor Sebastián for help

(C)

María dies maimed by her disease and abandoned by all but doctor

87

As with María, contact with the Gamallo series mediates the events of the rest of his life. But more than is so for her, it demonstrates the coupling noted by Ricardo Gullón of the game with Gamallo's subsequent attempts for revenge. Sequences I and II clearly relate to the game and its effect on Sebastián's life. His contact with María during the contest moves him to plan his first attempt to change his situation. María's subsequent flight with the card player, an action that ironically parallels his own planned escape with her, deals him a telling psychological blow. Rather than changing his condition, it only sinks him deeper into a state of frustration and depression. The remainder of his life is spent thinking of the past, or attempting to regain it in some vicarious way as is the case with his care for María and her son, manifested in IIB. This is intensified in IIIA, for the doctor's later years after the war approach a state of almost complete emotional paralysis. His existence is now reduced to drinking and remembering. In a manner similar to María, this psychological condition results in a virtual physical stasis and isolation.

Sequence III also associates Daniel with the end result of the bellicose situation precipitated by Gamallo's second attempt at revenge. The disturbed child, now an adult, is placed under his care after the war. As shall be seen below, his patient's mental state is attributable to the loss of his mother who abandoned him during the war. Marré Gamallo's visit brings him into contact with another person whose destiny is tied to the consequences of a parent's acts. The juxtaposition of the two characters (Marré and patient) is immediately responsible for Daniel Sebastián's death. The child, thinking Marré is his mother, becomes enraged when he sees her depart, and kills the doctor in his fury.

Therefore, as was the case with the María Timoner series, the structure of the *histoire* once again plots a one-directional flow for the doctor's life as a result of his association with the Gamallo sequence. That situation leads him to a desolate and isolated existence, in which he does nothing more than drink and recapitulate the past. It also accounts, years later, for his death.

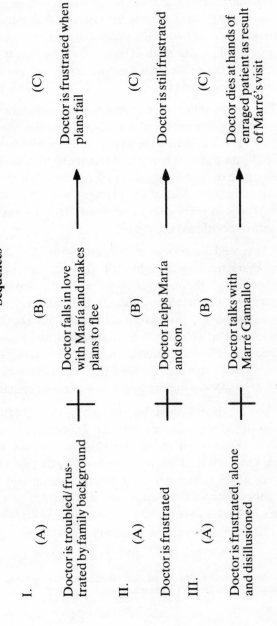

**Schematic IV
Doctor Sebastián
Series of
Sequences**

I. (A)

Doctor is troubled/frustrated by family background

(B)

Doctor falls in love with María and makes plans to flee

(C)

Doctor is frustrated when plans fail

II. (A)

Doctor is frustrated

(B)

Doctor helps María and son.

(C)

Doctor is still frustrated

III. (A)

Doctor is frustrated, alone and disillusioned

(B)

Doctor talks with Marré Gamallo

(C)

Doctor dies at hands of enraged patient as result of Marré's visit

The Marré Gamallo series consists of four sequences, as Schematic V shows. For several reasons her fate, like that of the doctor, is linked to the two coupled events alluded to numerous times above: the card game and its aftermath. The *histoire* manifests this through the way it relates her to the two other characters who are fundamentally important in the course of her life: her father and Luis I. Timoner.

The two components of proposition IA underscore the vital role of her father's actions. Ironically, Gamallo's own youth shapes his daughter's life. The officer, perhaps because of his psychological state induced by the game, or because of his childhood, affords his daughter the same type of upbringing he himself received.[9] He thus perpetuates a situation similar to the kind he endured, and opens Marré up to the same feelings of repression he suffered. They inevitably shape the structure of her life as they did his.

The second component of IA is also essential. Perhaps more than on any character, outside of himself, Gamallo's attempt at collective revenge through the medium of the war tells heaviest on his own daughter. For it is the military importance he achieves, in what is really a personal vendetta, that makes her a useful hostage for the Loyalist forces in Región. This significantly alters her life. In the first place it heightens the situation expressed in the first component of IA, in that Gamallo's lack of concern for her only intensifies her chilhood alienation from him. More importantly it facilitates her contact with Luis.

The time spent with María's son during the war (IB) functions as a happy interlude that brackets the frustration, oppression, and unhappiness that underscore her existence before and after this period. Thus, it is the knowledge, or memory that something better is possible, which incites her to attempt to regain that happiness by fleeing the existence imposed on her in IIIB. Ironically it is this very action which leads to her demise. This attempt (IVB) ultimately turns out to be an unsuccessful modification. While there is some sense of

9.   A comparison of pp. 69-72, treating Gamallo's youth, and those dealing with his daughter's (pp. 257-270) demonstrates this.

Schematic V
Marré Gamallo
**Series of
Sequences**

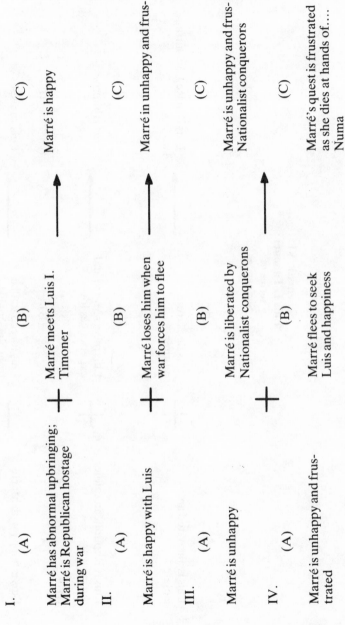

	(A)	(B)	(C)
I.	Marré has abnormal upbringing; Marré is Republican hostage during war	Marré meets Luis I. Timoner	Marré is happy
II.	Marré is happy with Luis	Marré loses him when war forces him to flee	Marré in unhappy and frustrated
III.	Marré is unhappy	Marré is liberated by Nationalist conquerons	Marré is unhappy and frustrated Nationalist conquerors
IV.	Marré is unhappy and frustrated	Marré flees to seek Luis and happiness	Marré's quest is frustrated as she dies at hands of.... Numa

91

Schematic VI
Luis I. Timoner
Series of
Sequences

1.

(A)   (B)   (C)

Luis is alienated and isolated   +   Luis flees from mother   →   Luis is in Región during war

II.

(A)   (B)   (C)

Luis is Republican soldier during war   +   Luis meets Marré and experiences love   →   Luis is happy

III.

(A)   (B)   (C)

Luis is happy with Marré   +   Luis forced to flee from Nationalist offensive   →   Luis vanishes release in the very act of leaving her repressive home environment, structurally it leads only to her death.

In certain ways, the propositions dealing with her and Luis (IIBC, IIIAB) represent a structural duplication of her relationship with Gamallo. María's son, like the officer, is another figure who ties her to both the card game and its aftermath, and the events of the war. Additionally, their relationship is in itself a doubling of the one between María and the officer. Luis' flight, and its effect on Marré, recalls a similar situation a generation earlier. Although undertaken for entirely different reasons, his flight parallels his mother's escape with the card player. The impact of these crises on the other member of the couple is also brutally clear, and the psychological importance of each of them has been amply demonstrated. It is interesting to note that there is a role reversal in the second generation, as first a female and then a male leaves; but still the filial ties are maintained. In both cases it is the Timoner member of the pair that departs.

From the above it is clear that, as was the case with the other series of the *histoire* already examined, Marré's fate is conditioned by her contact with events that so many times before have proved to be crucial for the text's actantial level. Her post-war experiences (IIBC, III, IV) represent intensified repetitions of her initial situation. Liberation by the Nationalists in IIIB is so in name only, since it propels her into a situation that is the polar opposite of the freedom she felt during her short period with Luis. Her attempt to change her fate, as has been noted, leads but to the final tragedy that the key moments of the Gamallo series conditioned: her death at the hands of el Numa's carbine.

The sequences documenting Luis I. Timoner's participation in the action of the *histoire* (see Schematic VI) portray the same symptoms of alienation and depression seen in other sequences. The direct cause of his symptoms is his mother's disease, for this accounts for their living in virtual isolation, attended only by Dr. Daniel Sebastián during infrequent visits. He, like his mother, experiences the inexorable spiral of physical isolation and mental depression. His condition in IA is indirectly attributable to the card game, since it was this event that precipitated his mother's flight and her isolated existence. Here, as with Marré, its effects are filtered through a second generation. If the officer's daughter is indelibly marked by the psychological and physical scars that her father received in the card game, so too is María's offspring. This isolation and frustration are clearly manifested in IA. Proposition IB represents an attempt to change that situation.[10] At the level of physical action it does accomplish its goal, since it displaces him from his mother's side to Región. Nevertheless, it produces another, unforeseeable change. His contact with Marré during the war (IIB) starts a fleeting interlude of happiness (IIC, IIIA) that the war takes away from him. As the Nationalist troops close in on Región, Luis flees, and his subsequent fate is unclear.

Hence, the war offers him a paradoxical situation similar to that of his lover. It puts him in contact with Marré, thus portending the chance for happiness, only to take this hope away by forcing him to flee into oblivion. Once again the linked presence of the card game and the war exact their toll on a character, bending his life in a one-way direction with no hope offered of any possibility to reverse it.

In Luis' case, the modifying situations in the first and third sequences underlie the one-way nature of the actions described there. Physical displacement is possible, but it cannot secure happiness.

10. The principal motivation for this action is Luis' having seen, for the first and only time, his mother's mutilated face that she had hidden behind a veil for years. The incident is described in the following manner:

   De debajo del mueble solamente sobresalía una pequeña y arrugada cabeza como la de esa tortuga que en posición invertida ya no pugna por enderezarse y ahora todo movimiento para prolongar una agonía cierta; se había desprendido su velo y —encaramado en el armario— el hijo de María vio por primera y última vez la cara de su madre: nada más que dos ojos desmesurados, verdosos y alucinantes, alojados en ese montón de podredumbre de que extraían su alimento. Luego tres pasos, tres patadas furiosas y un grito de estupor serán suficientes para lanzarle a esa carrera desenfrenada y fatídica, ese interminable viaje a la noche del odio y la soledad para huir de cuanto le rodea y olvidar la faz de su madre, sepultada bajo el armario, la mano crispada sobre la moneda de oro, convertida por la enfermedad de una sangrienta calavera salpicada de mordeduras negruzcas, dos bolas luminosas encima de un boquete que despedía un intenso tufo de mucosidades (p. 277).

What is more, it results only in the necessity of another dislocation, this time under circumstances that augur scant hope of modifying the character's initial situation.[11]

Dr. Daniel Sebastián's disturbed patient is the only major character whose life is not affected by the events of the card game. He can thus be construed as the antithesis of the card player whose life is deeply involved in the game but who is untouched by the other of the paired events that is critical to the novel's action: the war. The latter touches the child/patient in a very special and profound way. This is evident from the initial proposition of the first sequence and throughout the series (see Schematic VII). The child's mother, for reasons never completely explained, is forced to leave him in the care of a housekeeper during the war. She never returns and this abandonment leads to the child's depression and frustration (IC, IIA).

The approach of Marré's vehicle, very similar to the black one in which his mother departed years before, excites him into the belief that she has finally returned. But rather than modifying his initial condition, IIB —like IB— only heightens it. His frustration turns to rage when Marré departs in the black car that he thought was finally bringing a release from his long wait. It is in this state that he kills Daniel Sebastián, who goes to his patient's room to attempt to calm him down. The child's third attempt to modify his situation also proves futile (IIIB), for while he is able to vent his rage by killing the doctor, that action offers him no relief. Thus, at the end of the narrative discourse, the child is the only major character introduced into the *histoire* who is not accounted for by either disappearence or death. Clearly he is a survivor in name only. He now roams the doctor's house in a rage induced by the event that ultimately causes the deaths of the others. The very special nature of the patient's relationship with the war underscores its importance in his life. He, like others, is deeply

11. The finality of Luis' second escape is underscored by the fact that he is fleeing not only from the impending Nationalist victory but may, in fact, be fleeing the Loyalists as well. The possibility of Luis' desertion is alluded to on p. 277. This fact, if true, stresses the difficulty of the situation the war presented for him.

Schematic VII
Disturbed Child
Series of
Sequences

I.

(A)

Child is frustrated because mother is forced to leave him

+

(B)

Child becomes patient in Doctor Sebatián's sanatorium after the war

→

(C)

Child is frustrated beause mother has not returned

II.

(A)

Child is frustrated and disturbed

+

(B)

Approach of Marré's black car makes him believe mother has returned, and he becomes excited

→

(C)

Child is frustrated and enraged when car leaves

III.

(A)

Child is frustrated and enraged

+

(B)

In his fury child kills Doctor Sebastián

→

(C)

Child is enraged and alone

wounded by it. But at the same time, this victim is transformed into its unwitting henchman when he kills another victim of the war's effect. If the doctor was emotionally "dead" as a result of the linked pair of actions represented by the game/war, his ultimate physical demise is brought about by the same cause that drives his murderer insane.

Many critics have observed that *Volverás a Region* is the fictional creation of Juan Benet that provides the most comprehensive thematic coverage of the Spanish Civil War. At the level of content, this assertion is certainly correct. The text obviously provides an elaborate fictionalization of the events of this important period of Spanish history. My analysis of the *histoire* and its structure, however, clearly shows that viewed from this angle it is not his presentation of the details of the war itself that is the important item, but the effects that this event held out for those who were in some way touched by it. In structural terms, the *histoire* accentuates this by means of the way in which the two key events in its development (the card game and the war itself) affect all the characters who have a significant existence within the narrative discourse.

More specifically, it is the Gamallo series of sequences that accomplishes this and subsumes all the other series to it. The officer is, in essence, the *histoire*'s actantial fulcrum. His comportment in the card game, and his attempt to obtain revenge on a societal level through the medium of the Civil War, drastically alter the fate of all who come into contact with him, or who are in some way involved in the key actions cited above.

Almost magnetically, the characters' fates congeal around these paired acts, forming the intricate web visualized in Schematic I. The intersection of sequences associating them with the Gamallo series, however, begins to unravel the web until it becomes completely and irreversibly unwound. From that point forward, the course of the *histoire* charts a one-war irreversible direction. The post-war period is seen as the space in which the sterile working-out of the process takes place. This is most vividly underscored if one examines the fate of the characters introduced in the various sequences that structure the *his-*

toire. All of them have now either disappeared (Luis), died (María, Gamallo, Daniel, Marré), or are in a state of mental disorder (the doctor's patient). The manner in which they are withdrawn from the action serves to emphasize the inevitability of their destinies. Luis I. Timoner's final flight only intensifies and in no way improves his initial situation. The particularly violent or horrible deaths that await the majority of the participants in the text's action are also indicative of this fact. The only remaining survivor is one in name only. If the war has finally become the cause of the others' loss of life, it offers him little better fate: mental disorder.

Seen in terms of its structure, the *histoire* is thus homologous to the anti-regime collective subject elaborated in Chapter I. Both view the post-war period as a space characterized by decadence and decay. This state, in both cases, is predicated on the same cause: the destructive effects that were the outcome of the Civil War.

II
Analysis of *Discours*
A. Introduction:
Narrative Macro-Units

As dictated by Genette's methodology, the most substantial portion of this section is given over to the study of how the *histoire* is manifested in the *discours*, and the ideological implications of this structural relationship. The *histoire*, nevertheless, is not the only constituent unit of the *discours*. In addition to the *histoire*, I have isolated three other macro-compositional units which merit attention. Each of them will be briefly sketched below. The manner in which these entities are enclosed in the physical text that one reads between the covers of the book entitled *Volverás a Región* presents structural complexities that tax the literary competence of even the best reader to make coherent the maze-like structure of this challenging narrative discourse.

Before proceeding, however, a word must be said about the physical divisions introduced in the text. Genette contends in "Discours du récit" that narrative structure need not be subsumed to such artificial boundaries as chapter or sub-chapter divisions. Sections of the *discours*, or of its components, need not stop or start at physical junctions in the text. To a certain extent this view holds for *Volverás a Región*. Yet in Benet's first novel, external constraints are important if only to facilitate reference to the dispersion and distribution of the elements of the *discours* within the text. My insistence on this factor is attributable, in addition to concerns for clarity, to the fact that in early versions of the novel these separations did not exist. As Benet recounts in his essay "Breve historia de *Volverás a Región*," it was only at the urging of his friends, who thought the monolithic block of earlier versions too inaccessible, that he introduced divisions into the text.[12] Still it is not surprising that the breaks he did include in the published version represent important moments of beginning, closure, and reorientation. Those instances where these junctures play a crucial role will be discussed in the course of this section.

The physical text itself is separated into four large units or chapters, each marked with a Roman numeral. Each major division is further sub-divided through the use of a series of stars placed in the middle of the page. I have arbitrarily assigned each of these sub-chapters an Arabic numeral (see Schematic VIII). I have chosen the Roman/ Arabic alternation to avoid confusion with the sequences of the *histoire*, which were labeled with a Roman numeral and a capital letter.

The Civil War

That portion of the text given over to the Spanish Civil War is the second most important element of the *discours*. The considerable space devoted to the description and analysis of battles and related political events has led critics to conclude that this is Benet's most comprehensive treatment of the period. This portrait has a significance I would not wish to deny. One of the major reasons the portrayal of the war is so striking is the manner in which Benet constructs this part of the text's macro-structure. He shrewdly places his fictionalization of the war in a far-off corner of the peninsula within a paradigmatic framework of references relating to key events in the real conflict, thereby providing an element of verisimilitude to the discussion of the

---

12. ...suprimí todo un pasaje que resultaba muy dudoso (la historia de un niño que abandonado en un internado de religiosas para entretenerse creaba tal cizaña que toda la comunidad terminaba por morder el polvo o ahorcar los hábitos o caer en brazos de los más abominables pecados), dividí en conjunto en cuatro capítulos... (pp. 163-164).

war in Región. The text itself explains that the war in that area is a paradigmatic representation of the entire conflict, a kind of microcosmic view of it.[13]

Schematic VIII
External Divisions
of
Physical Text

Chapter I (7-90)	Chapter II (91-179)	Chapter III (180-258)	Chapter IV (259-315)
Part 1 (7-15)	Part 1 (91-120)	Part 1 (180-234)	Part 1 (259-285)
Part 2 (15-27)	Part 2 (120-149)	Part 2 (234-254)	Part 2 (285-293)
Part 3 (27-35)	Part 3 (149-177)	Part 3 (255-258)	Part 3 (293-311)
Part 4 (35-41)	Part 4 (177-179)		Part 4 (312-315)
Part 5 (51-73)			
Part 6 (73-90)			

13. Todo el curso de la guerra civil en la comarca de Región empieza a verse claro cuando se comprende que, en más de un aspecto, es un paradigma a escala mayor y a un ritmo más lento de los sucesos peninsulares (p. 75).

Exemplary of this tactic is the considerable space in I,6 devoted to Gamallo's plan for conquering Región. His strategy is meshed with the overall Nationalist plan for a war of attrition, in an attempt not only to win the war, but the peace as well, by insuring the complete decimation of the opponent. The *Plan Gamallo* is also linked to Rebel Spain's propagandistic ploys, here seen in the practice of substituting the foreign troops that had done much of its fighting with less offensive and more *castizo* ones, especially at key moments of the conflict, such as the taking of key Republican cities.

Todas las ofensivas, si se pueden llamar así, que se plantearán en la primavera y verano del año 38 se traducirán, por deseo expreso del Mando, en batallas de usura, en ataques frontales con los que desgastar los cuadros —los cuadros de campo sustituidos a menudo por oficiales políticos—, en largas campañas de inútil atracción al único objeto de prolongar hasta sus últimas consecuencias una guerra concluida con un plantel de vencedores demasiado numeroso e inquietante. Los italianos del C.T.V. (en el momento en que se podía extraer sus largas espinas) y las divisiones marroquíes —todos los políticamente inofensivos— son apresurada e inexplicablemente retirados de las primeras líneas para sustituirlos por unas formaciones frescas procedentes de Valladolid, de Galicia, de Navarra y del Maestrazgo, hombres que ocuparon jubilosos las trincheras y que —antes que el manejo de las armas— aprendieron a cantar a ensayar los aires triunfales con que dispusieron a hacer su entrada en Madrid, en Valencia y en Región (p. 65)

In addition to the linkage of the campaign in Región to specific political and tactical considerations that lay at the base of actual Nationalist strategy, its conquest is mentioned in the same sentence with those of Madrid and Valencia, the two successive capitals of the Second Spanish Republic. This association is calculated to enhance the importance of the fictional city. Similar references, linking Región to well-known battles, serve the same purpose. At one point, for instance, the text refers to the Republican strategy that led to defeat at such places as "...los campos del Jarama y el Tajo, en Brunete y en Teruel, en cierto modo prevaleció en una Región circundada de silenciosas montañas y pequeños prados..." (p. 75).

This paradigmatic association extends to other aspects of the portrayal of the war. The internal struggles of the various Loyalist factions resisting Gamallo's advance are at one point described in such a way as to associate the dispute with the one that raged in Madrid during the war's final moments, over whether to seek a negotiated settlement or to continue the struggle. "La negociación se hizo imposible —e inútiles todos sus esfuerzos y sacrificios— por la intransigencia de otros grupos que, engañados por su fuerza y por su credo, enarbolaron la insignia de su resistencia a ultranza sin pararse a pensar en su famosa invencibilidad" (p. 84).

While these examples demonstrate both the technique used to associate Región with the real war and Benet's knowledge of this period, we must keep in mind something that many of the critics surveyed in Chapter I did not. *Volverás a Región*, or any novel dealing with the Civil War, is not an essay, and its content will not necessarily reveal a true picture of the author's world view. In Benet's case, those desiring a truer assessment of his view of the war's battles would be far better off reading the monograph *¿Qué fue de la guerra civil?* than this novel. Also, the amount of space directly related to the war is substantially attenuated if it is remembered that much of this material is subsumed to the sequences of the *histoire*. Hence the plan formulated by Gamallo, while presented as an interesting counterpart to the Nationalist strategy, is more important for what it reveals about its planner's motivations and about the way in which the latter affects the structure of the narrative action.

Marré's connection to the portrayal of the Civil War stands in the same relationship to this element of the *discours* as does the Gamallo series. The portions of the text that treat her involvement are most meaningful for what they tell the reader about the effects of the conflict on her, and how this is translated into the structure of the *histoire*. The same type of observation may be made about the other main actors in the *histoire* who come into contact with the war: Luis I. Timoner, the disturbed child, and Dr. Sebastián.

Although it does not pose the problems of decipherment that the *histoire* does, the way in which the Civil War macro-element of the *discours* is inserted in the text is taxing. This is due to the fact that the description of the war is spread throughout the entire text. An event described in the first chapter, which contains in capsule form references to almost all the valuable information relating to the portrayal of the conflict, may be taken up again in the second chapter, and then again in subsequent ones. This is the case with the description of the final days before Región's capture by the Nationalists. This event is first described in I,6; again in II,4; and for a third and fourth time in IV,2 and IV,3. In addition, each successive reference adds information not found in the previous one. Such a method of presentation strains the reader's capacity for processing the narrative information he is receiving, for it forces him to have constantly in his grasp keys that will enable him to associate later references with those made perhaps two hundred pages before.

Narrative Space/Setting

The presentation of narrative space is composed both of descriptions of the area's imposing geo-climatic characteristics, and those elements which contribute to its pervasive "mythic" ambience. One of the most important components of the latter is the enigmatic figure of el Numa. Aspects of narrative space dealing with his role in the text both from an intertextual and a syntactical standpoint are discussed in detail in the following chapter, as are certain specific aspects of Región's geography that critics have associated with its "mythic" qualities.[14]

---

14. I have dealt with Región's imposing physical geography and climate, their possible source, and the meaning attributable to the structure of this presentation in "Región's Brazilian Backlands.

Background Information/Description

Under this heading are grouped those portions of the *discours* not directly concerned with any of the other three. Examples would be background information dealing with the history of Región before the main sequences of the *histoire* begin, or with such figures as the card player and the *barquera*. I view this category as supportive of the other three.

B. Temporal Consideration:
Order

Of the three categories Genette groups under the heading of *temps, ordre* is the most important for my analysis since it is most directly related to the syntactical disposition of the sequences of the *histoire* in the *discours*. In studying the order of a narrative text the first step is to establish the base unit, or narrative present, from which all analeptic and proleptic movement can be measured.[14bis] In *Volverás a Región* this unit encompasses the actions that take place from Marré Gamallo's arrival in Región to visit Dr. Daniel Sebastián and inquire about Luis I. Timoner, to her departure and the subsequent deaths of both her and the doctor. The base incorporates sequences from the

---

14 bis. Julia Lupinacci Wescott's recent "Exposition and Plot in Benet's *Volverás a Región*," *Kentucky Romance Quarterly*, 28 (1981), 155-163, also focuses on the peculiarities of the text's narrative arrangement. Using a model rooted in Meir Sternberg's "What is Exposition?" in *The Theory of the Novel*, ed. John Halperin (New York: Oxford University Press, 1974) Wescott analyzes aspects of what in this chapter are considered in the sections dedicated to the syntactical disposition of the *histoire* in the *discours*. She concludes that the "final effect of Benet's inverted technique, however, is an oblique sharpening of the reader's focus on the novel's central themes of predetermination and death because, in a sense, it embodies them," (p. 162). Her useful study, then, explores some of the same techniques discussed here, but not in the same depth. Its conclusions as to the ideological subtext motivating the narrative arrangement employed in *Volverás a Región*, moreover, differ widely from my own.

various series studied in the first part of this chapter, specifically: II and III of the disturbed child series; III of the Daniel Sebastián series; and IV of the Marré Gamallo series.

The manner in which the base unit is inserted in the *discours* is indicative of the overall problem posed by the disposition of the *histoire* in the *discours*. The first reference to it begins I,2 of the text.

> En aquella ocasión no se trataba de una vieja camioneta cargada de bultos y cuerdas sino de un coche negro, de modelo antiguo pero con empaque. No por eso, ni el hecho de ser conducido por una mujer, despertó la curiosidad de los que lo vieron pasar a la caída de la tarde, un día dorado de septiembre, sublimación, éxtasis y agonía de un verano sediento y de un anhelo de agua; más bien vino a aumentar el recelo por los extraños y la confianza en su tierra, capaz de atraer hacia su fin a un género de personas hasta entonces nunca vistas.
>
> Un día del antiguo verano había llegado hasta su casa un coche semejante.... (p. 15).

The passage quoted taxes the comprehensive skills of even the best reader from the start. References to repeated visits by black automobiles, and the "aquella ocasión" are perplexing because they have no antecedent: there is as yet no context in which to process this information. From the study of the *histoire*, it is known that the woman arriving in the black car is Marré Gamallo, returning to Región to recapture her past; but, in fact, her identity is withheld until much later in the *discours*. The figure watching the approach of the car is the disturbed child who associates its return with a similar black car in which his mother departed years before (hence the reference to the car he saw in the "antiguo verano"). As with Marré's identity, the reader is puzzled because neither the disturbed child witnessing the return nor departure years before has any context. Information pertaining to the child however, is not postponed long, for the pages directly following his introduction explain sequences I and II of the series dealing with him.

The second reference to the text's narrative present occurs seventy-six pages later at another juncture in the physical text (the beginning of Chapter II), and pertains to the black car mentioned on page fifteen. "Ciertamente era un coche parecido, del mismo color negro, a aquél en que se había marchado su madre al principio de la guerra" (p. 91). What is interesting is that this passage, which seems directly linked both syntactically and conceptually to one of the two statements about cars examined above, actually takes place prior to the scene described in the first paragraph of page fifteen. That this is so is apparent when the reader learns that the child had been watching the parked car all afternoon, while in the previous reference, the car was observed at the *close* of the afternoon. As Marré returns to the car and prepares to drive to the doctor's clinic, the child runs to tell him of her impending visit, thinking that his mother has returned (pp. 91-92). Three pages later, the doctor goes to the door to observe the road for any sign of the car: "Se levantó con lentitud, se acercó a la otra ventana que estaba cerrada, abrió el frailero y observó con parsimonia el tramo de la carretera" (p. 95). He then takes the child upstairs to his room, calms him, and puts him to bed. Daniel returns downstairs, peers out the window again to see the arrival of Marré's auto, her exit from it, and her approach to the house; he then hears the doorbell (p. 96). He tries to ignore her arrival (p. 97) but is unable to, because the patient upstairs has seen her approach, and, sure that it is his mother, starts to scream (p. 97). Sebastián goes upstairs and gives him an injection to sedate him (pp. 97-98), comes down, and finally opens the door (p. 98).

The conversation sustained that night by Daniel and Marré occupies pp. 98-312. Periodic sections break off this conversation as the narrator inserts related material. Their conversation is also punctuated by Marré's questions as to the identity of the person shouting upstairs (pp. 201, 202, 245). The action of the base sequence continues on p. 312 which is, significantly, the beginning of the final portion of the physical text: IV, 4. Having fallen asleep the doctor is awakened ("no era aún de día cuando el Doctor despertó") to find that Marré has just departed ("se levantó inquieto pero antes de llegar a la mesa tropezó un par de veces con sus zapatillas. Entonces le llegó el ruido del motor y un reflejo del resplandor de los faros asomó por el ventanal"). He then hears the child's renewed movement, sparked by the car's departure. He goes upstairs to try to calm him, and assure him that the person who has left was not his mother: "—No, no era ella. Espera. Te digo que no era ella. Créeme. ¿Cómo crees que te iba...?" (p. 314). In his rage, the child kills Daniel (p. 314), and for what is left of the night, rampages through the house shouting and venting his frustration on the furniture and windows (p. 315). The action of the narrative present concludes with a reference to a far-off report of el Numa's carbine signaling Marré's death, and the reestablishment of Región's solitude. "Hasta que, con las luces del día, entre dos ladridos de un perro solitario, el eco de un disparo lejano vino a restablecer el silencio habitual del lugar" (p. 315).

The insertion of the base unit in the text highlights many of the analytical and interpretative problems posed by the placement of each of the *histoire*'s series of sequences in the *discours*. On the interpretive level the fundamental difficulty is the non-sequential and non-chronological presentation of the material. A study of the base sequence clearly indicates this. Here the end and/or the effects of the process are revealed first, the beginning and/or the causes being postponed. The significance of this is that the reader is unable to measure with any certainty the importance of a given event, because the contextual information needed to complete the process is presented later. This forces the reader to retain large amounts of narrative information and for pages on end until clarification appears in the text that will allow comprehension of what has been read. The manner in which the material dealing with the disturbed child is presented is one example of this. First the reader learns that his mother left him years ago. Only after this fact is introduced is the material detailing the reasons for her departure, the significance of this event for his life, and how he came to be at the doctor's clinic presented. With Doctor Sebastián and Marré Gamallo, the situation is even more difficult. At least with the distrubed child the material that fills in the gaps is presented soon after his introduction. Marré's identity, like the doctor's remains a mystery for many pages after they are introduced in the base sequence. It is only with great difficulty that the reader is able to piece together their identities, and make sense of the fragmented manner in which their lives are presented.

Another problem related to coherence that is attested to by the base sequence is the use of multiple references to similar but different objects or persons. The most obvious example of this is the problem of the black cars. Another is the confusion caused by the fact that there are three female characters with the name Adela: the maid who cares for the disturbed child during the war; the woman usually referred to as Muerte, who runs the hotel in which Marré stays in the war's waning days, and the wife of the enigmatic doctor Rumbal. All this serves to place more difficulties in the path of the reader who must constantly scurry to find out which of the women is being referred to in any given situation.

At the analytical level the fact that the base unit spans almost the entire physical text presents a problem with regard to the proleptic or analeptic nature of the rest of the *histoire*. Seen in terms of the narrative present the rest of the sequences of the *histoire* represent analeptical insertions to fill in the material that leads to the narrative present. At the same time, because of the non-sequential insertion of each of the propositions of any given sequence into the structure of the *discours*, these individual propositions could be viewed as proleptic within the syntagma of that series.

Schematic IX represents a glossing of references to the sequences of the *histoire* as they are introduced in the text from its beginning to its conclusion. A perusal of the Schematic bears out that, as was the case with the base unit, almost all the sequences are presented in a non-chronological order. This is seen in the fact that for any given series, sequence I is normally not the first one introduced. A close analysis of Schematic IX reveals another key fact: the first propositions of the *histoire* inserted in the *discours* provide anticipatory allusions to critical moments of the narrative action. They represent proleptic references to sequences that will be explained later. In effect they

Schematic IX

Disposition of Elements of *Histoire*

in *Discours* by Linear Insertion

Gamallo IABC/IIBC(11-12)	Doctor IIIA (13)	Gamallo IIB (15) María IB	Marré IVB (15-19)
Child IIB/IC (15)	Child IA (19)	Child IB (27)	Gamallo IIB (34) María IB
Luis IIA (36)	Gamallo IIIAB (54-67)	Gamallo IIAB (72-73)	Gamallo IIIB (80-90)
Gamallo IIIBC (89)	Child IIB (91)	Child IIB (91-93)	Doctor IIIA (93)
Doctor IB (94)	Doctor IIIA (94-95)	Doctor IIIA (96-102)	Marré ABC (104)
Gamallo IBC/IIB María IB		Marré IVB Child IIB	
Doctor IIA (106)	Luis IIB (109) Marré IIBC	Doctor IBC/IIABC(110-111) María IBC/IIABC	Doctor IA (121-135)
María IIIA (136)	Doctor IIC (136) Gamallo IIB	Doctor IA (137-139)	Doctor IIIA (141-149)
Marré IAB (149-157)	Marré IIIC (158)	Marré IABC/IIABC/IIIABC (158-177)	
Child IA (178-179)	Gamallo IBC/IIBC (184-185)	Gamallo IIA (201)	Gamallo IIB (204-207)
Gamallo IIB (207)	Doctor IA (217)	Doctor IIB (220)	Gamallo IIB (221)
Gamallo IIB (223-234)	Doctor IB (234-236)	María IA (236-240) Gamallo IB	Doctor IB (241)
Gamallo IBC (243-244)	Gamallo IIAB (245)	Child IIC (245)	
Marré IB (260)	Marré IA (261)	Gamallo IB (262)	Doctor IBC (255-259) Marré IB (262)
Marré IA (264)	Marré IVAB (265)	Marré IB (266)	Gamallo IIIB (267)
Marré IA (267-273)	Luis IABC/IIA/IIIBC (275-277)	Marré IA (278)	Marré IVA (279)
Marré IA (280-283)	Gamallo IIIC (286)	Marré IC/IIA (298) Luis IIC Marré IIAB (307-308) Luis IIIB	Marré IVAB (300-302)
Marré IIA (304)	Marré IIIB (306)	Marré IIIC (315)	Marré IIAB (308-310)
Doctor IIIC (314) Child IIIB	Child IIIC (315)		

serve an annunciatory function, focusing our attention from the start on those instances that organize and order the action of the *histoire*, but they cause the same problems of comprehension and coherence noticed in my explanation of the base sequence. At the very start of the text the reader is presented crucial information that is unintelligible until much later. Clarification of these instances is often delayed so long that, by the time explanatory information is introduced, the reader may well have forgotten the bits of information previously presente. Thus those proleptic clues to the narrative's significance may now be lost.

With this technique in mind it is quite significant that the first reference to the *histoire* is the following:

Tal vez la decadencia empieza una mañana de las postrimerías del verano con una reunión de militares, jinetes y rastreadores dispuestos a batir el monte en busca de un jugador de fortuna, el donjuán extranjero que una noche de casino se levantó con su honor y su dinero; la decadencia no es más que eso, la memoria y la polvareda de aquella cabalgata por el camino del Torce, el frenesí de una sociedad agotada y dispuesta a creer que iba a recobrar el honor ausente en una barraca de la sierra, un montón de piezas de nácar, y una venganza de sangre. A partir de entonces la polvareda se transforma en pasado y el pasado en honor: la memoria es un dedo tembloroso que unos años más tarde descorrerá los estores agujereados de la ventana del comedor para señalar la silueta orgullosa, temible y lejana del Monje donde, al parecer, han ido a perderse y concentrarse todas las ilusiones adolescentes que huyeron con el ruido de los caballos y los carruajes, que resucitan enfermos con el sonido de los motores y el eco de los disparos, mezclado al silbido de las espadañas al igual que en los días finales de aquella edad sin razón quedó unido al sonido acerbo y evocativo de triángulos y xilófonos (pp. 11-12).

The first lines of this passage intimate that Región's decadence is related to a card game and to a subsequent chase. As the reader first processes this information it means little to him. But many of the pieces of information presented initially here will be repeated on numerous occasions. Examples include the mountain chase (*cabalgata* and *polvareda*) and the chips used in the card game (*piezas de nácar*) between Gamallo and his unknown opponent, here referred to as the "donjuán extranjero" or "jugador de fortuna". All of this refers to material analyzed in detail in the first section of this chapter: the card game in Región's casino, the maiming inflicted upon Gamallo at its conclusion, and the mountain chase carried out to exact revenge and recover María Timoner. This information is contained in propositions IIBC of the Gamallo series. As I explained in Section I of this chapter these propositions represent the first of Gamallo's paired attempts at revenge. The second, of course, is his action during the Civil War, and the two spur the one-directional flow of the *histoire*. With this in mind it is noteworthy that the end of the quoted material, although it does not refer to a specific proposition of the *histoire*, does establish a cause/effect relationship between the card game and the chase and the war, "edad sin razón;" whose shrill martial music "sonido acerbo y evocativo de triángulos y xilófonos" stands in marked contrast to the silence and desolation of post-war Región, a condition directly attributable to the effects of the war.

The link between the card game, chase and war as cause and post-war Región as the effect of these actions is supported through the insertional order of propositions of the *histoire* in the *discours*. After the reference to the game and the chase, the next occurrence of the *histoire* deals with the post-war desolation of the area, specifically to Dr. Sebastián's sitting alone in his clinic at some unspecified moment before the arrival of Marré Gamallo. "Con los ojos cerrados su mano abre un cajón lleno de viejas fotografías amarillentas, borlones de seda y bandas de raso de una congregación desaparecida para extraer, de una vieja caja de frutas donde guarda los retazos un pequeño trozo de cuerda satinada por el uso y anudado en varios puntos como un rosario, en el que, con un gesto diestro y rápido, hace una nueva cuenta cuando el sonido del motor alcanza sus oídos" (p. 13). Action then switches back to the card game and chase and their effects, when the following reference to the *histoire* is presented a page later: "...todas las ilusiones y promesas rotas por la polvareda de los jinetes que con la distancia y el tiempo aumentarán de tamaño hasta convertir en grandeza y honor lo que no fue en su día sino ruindad y orgullo, pobreza y miedo" (p. 14). The next insertion draws the reader to the post-war period (effects) in the form of the action in which the disturbed child sees the approach of Marré Gamallo's black vehicle (p. 15).

The order in which this information is presented underscores from the very beginning of the text the key events of the *histoire*. First mentioned are the card game and the chase, which, as has been demonstrated, change the course of the narrative action, and are directly associated in the *histoire* with Gamallo's attempt to obtain revenge on the societal level years later. The reader's attention is then brought back to the war's effects by means of a reference to the doctor's solitary existence in post-war Región. After a second reference to the card game, the effects are presented again. This time, however, the text has arrived at the beginning of the narrative present which ends with the destruction of two of the three remaining survivors of the *histoire*. The establishment of this contrapuntal cause/effect relationship and the association at the beginning of the text of references to key elements of the *histoire* (card game/war/post-war ruin/narrative present) focus from the start on those elements that are to be crucial to the narrative action and highlight them by giving them a preferential placement at the beginning of the *discours*.

The first reference to most of the other characters in the *histoire* also establishes a linkage to either the card game, the war, or the post-war period, in this way underscoring the importance of those events already afforded a significant position in the *discours*. The Marré series is introduced by two insertions of the IVB proposition (her trip back to post-war Región in search of her past). The first appears on p. 15, the second occurs with her arrival at the doctor's house (pp. 96-106). This is followed by a reference to the second sequence of her series, dealing with her life during the final days of the war (p. 104). and by a more detailed reference to her final days with Luis Timoner (p. 109).

113

The first time the doctor's series appears, it deals concretely with sequence III (p. 13, p. 91). The next reference (p. 94) recounts his involvement in the card game, its effects on him (p. 100), and his futile search for María Timoner at its conclusion (pp. 110-111). The same technique is evident in the disturbed child series. The reader is provided first with a reference to his life in post-war Región (p. 15), but the action involving him then shifts back to the bellicose period in order to explain his condition (pp. 15-27). A striking parallel is perceptible in this arrangement. The first propositions mentioned in the *discours* serve to determine how the sequences for most of the key figures of the *histoire* are ordered. The sequences too begin with one of the crucial moments of the narrative action which constitute, as has been seen, the first elements introduced into the *discours*.

In addition to initial placement, another ordering process through which key elements of the *histoire* are emphasized is repetition. This tactic is most evident with regard to the card game/Civil War pairing especially as it effects the Gamallo series. Schematic X illustrates this. I have glossed each proposition related to either unit of the pair. The number of references is conspicuous. Allusions to, or complete descriptions of the card game and chase occur at least twelve times in the course of the narrative (an average of one almost every thirty pages). Propositions mentioning the war and the revenge factor therein (IIIB) —exclusive of those referring to Gamallo's death (IIIC)— appear on at least five occasions. This repetitiveness has the effect of keeping before the reader references to those propositions that mediate the course of the action.

In my discussion of the base sequence I alluded to the analytical problems caused by the fact that the *discours'* narrative present spans almost the entire physical text. The displacement of this short time span through almost three hundred pages of text helps to define its analeptical nature. Several types of analepses are present. External ones go beyond the first propositions of each of the series of the *histoire* and flesh it out by adding completive information on events that transpire before the beginning of each sequence. Such analepses serve

114

Gamallo IBC/IIBC (11-12) (card game) (cabalgata/ revenge)	Gamallo IIB (14) (revenge/ cabalgata)	Gamallo IIB (34) (revenge/ cabalgata)	Gamallo IIIAB (54-67) (war)
Gamallo IIAB (68) (revenge/ cabalgata)	Gamallo IA (68-70) (youth)	Gamallo IB (70-71) (card game)	Gamallo IA (72-73) (youth)
Gamallo IIIB (80-90) (war/revenge)	Gamallo IIIC (89) (death)	Gamallo IBC/IIB (94) (card game/revenge/ cabalgata)	Gamallo IIB (136) (revenge/ cabalgata)
Gamallo IBC/IIBC (184-185) (revenge/cabalgata)	Gamallo IIB (204-207) (revenge/cabalgata)	Gamallo IIB (207) (revenge/cabalgata)	Gamallo IIB (221) (revenge/cabalgata)
Gamallo IIB (223-234) (revenge/cabalgata)	Gamallo IBC (236-240) (card game)	Gamallo IBC (243-244) (card game)	Gamallo IIAB (245) (revenge/cabalgata)
Gamallo IB (262) (card game)	Gamallo IIIB (267) (revenge/war)	Gamallo IIIC (286) (death)	

another function in that they mesh two macro-units of the *discours*: the *histoire* and the background information unit.

The majority of the analepses in the text are internal in nature. Completative ones function as their name suggests. They fill in, bit by bit, and in the disjointed manner in which the information in the *histoire* is related in the *discours*, those pieces of information that explain the lives and actions of the major participants after their sequences are initially presented. Repetitive analepses constantly recall incidents introduced earlier. The most obvious example of this type is the continual repetition of the key propositions of the Gámallo series studied above, but repetition also characterizes such situations as Marre's participation in the war, and Daniel's involvement in the card game, both elements being continually reintroduced as Schematic IX shows.

This analeptic ordering process is highly significant since it orients the *discours* in a retrospective manner. The narrative present represents the space in which Región's post-war decadence is explained through continual references to the past. Even more important is the almost dialectical relationship that exists between the proleptic references to the *histoire* inserted before the base unit begins, and the analeptic orientation of the action that unit provides. Once again the ordering process of the *discours* is seen to highlight key segments of the *histoire*, this time by funneling our perception of these propositions in a retrospective manner. The movement is from a decadent almost lifeless present backward toward an exploration of the causes of that decadence; and then back to the present, slowly filling in the information that explains Marré's and Daniel's recollections.

Seen in terms of its manifestation in the physical text, the *discours* is ordered in almost a circular manner. Because the short period of time encompassed by the base unit spans practically the whole text, the *discours* begins and ends at virtually the same place. Excluding the proleptic references, the text's action commences with the reference to the base unit on page fifteen (the beginning of section I,2). Directly preceding this, and closing section I, 1 of the narrative, is a reference to el Numa and his function: maintaining Región's hermetically sealed

116

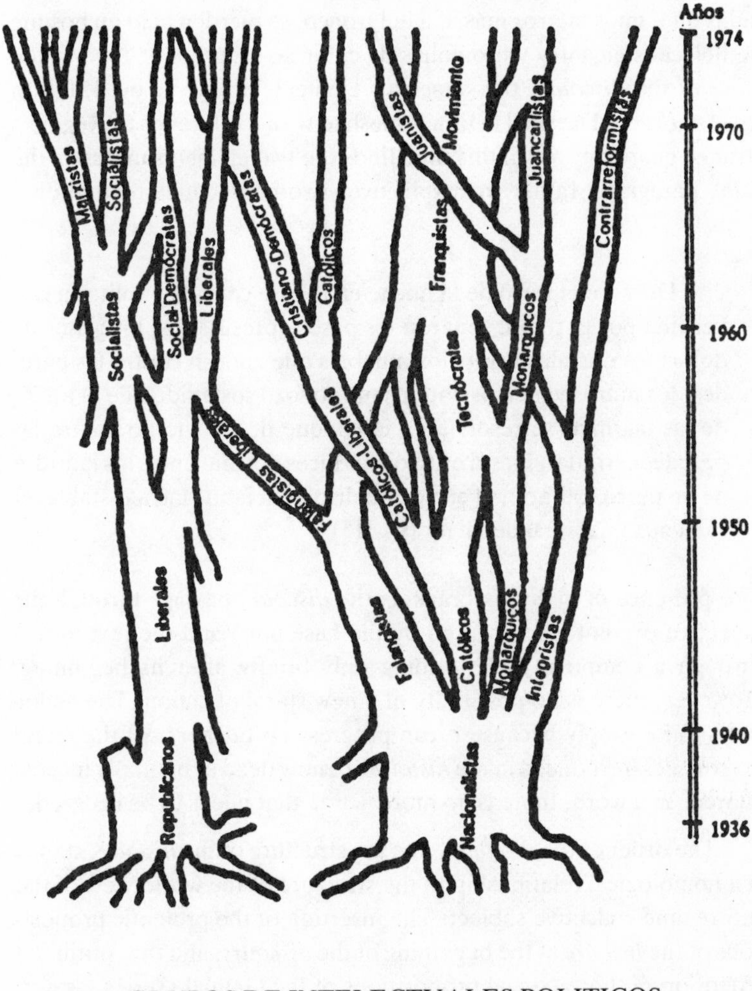

Años
1974
1970
1960
1950
1940
1936
Marxistas
Socialistas
Socialistas
Social-Demócratas
Liberales
Cristiano-Demócratas
Católicos
Juanistas
Movimiento
Juancarlistas
Contrarreformistas
Franquistas
Monárquicos
Tecnócratas
Católicos-Liberales
Falangistas Liberales
Liberales
Falangistas
Católicos
Monárquicos
Integristas
Republicanos
Nacionalistas

GRUPOS DE INTELECTUALES POLITICOS

isolation. "Sólo queda el silencio continental de la sierra, testimonio del disparo que un día lo desgarró, y las huellas de unas cubiertas gastadas que, unos metros más allá del tronco, se pierden bajo un bosque de helechos gigantes y bromelias de color de sangre" (p. 15). At the close of the *discours*, the same two elements are juxtaposed, but in reverse order. The final action is meshed with a reference to Región's strange guardian, which this time finds the two elements united in the same paragraph rather than split over two consecutive textual divisions.

> Durante el resto de la noche en la casa cerrada y solitaria casi vencida por la ruina, sonaron los pasos apresurados, los gritos de dolor, los cristales rotos, los muebles que chocan contra las paredes; los muros y hierros batidos, un sollozo sostenido que al límite de las lágrimas se resolvía en el choque de un cuerpo contra las paredes cerradas. Hasta que con las luces del día, entre los ladridos de un perro solitario, el eco de un disparo lejano vino a restablecer el silencio habitual del lugar (p. 315).

The presence of el Numa brackets the *discours* passage through the narrative present (represented by the base unit) and the text moves through a complete cycle, ending only briefly after its beginning. However, there is no possibility of a new spiral of action. The action stops quite simply because it can progress no further. All the major personages introduced in the *histoire* are now dead or mentally incapacitated. In a word, there is no more action that needs to be ordered.

The order of the *discours*, like the structure of the *histoire*, stands in a homological relationship to the structure of the world view of the anti-regime collective subject. The insertion of the proleptic propositions of the *histoire* at the beginning of the *discours*, and the continued repetition of those crucial propositions of the Gamallo series, as well as those dealing with other participants, emphasize the importance of these events as cause of post-war Región's decadence, a situation first mentioned in terms of the text's action when the reader sees Daniel Sebastián wasting away in Región (p. 13). The retrospective and circular characteristics of the ordering process, perceptible in the structure of the *discours*, underscore its orientation toward the past, and the futureless present in which this retrospective pondering takes place. These two elements, then, highlight the effects of the causes.

The homological relationship with the structure of the anti-regime collective subject is obvious. The latter, like the order of the *discours*, sees the war in terms of the effects it holds out for post-war Spain. The war opens an irreversible flow of decadence and decay that characterize both the francoist period of Spanish history, and the order in which the *discours* presents to the reader the action of the *histoire*.

C. Temporal Considerations:
Duration and Frequency

These two temporal aspects are less significant for the purposes of my analysis than is the syntactical order of the narrative. Still, they have a strategic role in that they intensify the ideological message that lies within the structure of the *discours*. This is accomplished through the manner in which they regulate the material being ordered.

Analytical problems analogous to those encountered in discussing the order of the *discours* appear again with respect to the latter's *durée*. As in the previous section, the cause is the large expanse of the *discours* occupied by the base unit, and the analeptical ordering processes that characterize it. The time of the base sequence, as has been noted, is something under one day —from Marré's arrival one September afternoon, till the following morning. The temporal field of the *histoire* as a whole ranges from some point in the early 1900's (Gamallo's and Sebastián's childhood), to the daughter's return to Región sometime in the 1960's. The base sequence, however, occupies almost the entire physical text, so that the very short relative time of narrative present brackets over three hundred pages of physical text. At the same time, the analeptical nature of this unit provides for continual reference to segments of the *histoire* that are presented in more and more detail, taking up, therefore, more space, and consequently having a longer duration. In this complex relationship several categories discussed by Genette are perceptible. Almost the entire narrative present is one prolonged scene or pseudo-scene, occupied by the monologue-like conversation between Marré and Daniel Sebastián. The first of the long sequences begins on page ninety-eight, and the last ends with the close of section IV,3 (p. 313). This present-time scene fades toward explicative elisions as Marré and Daniel switch from speaking directly to each other to ignoring their respective interlocutors and speaking about the past in a manner that becomes almost pure monologue. The elisions subtly advance the *discours* almost imperceptibly in relation to the expanse of the *histoire* they encompass in the characters' successive recollections of their pasts.

The remainder of the base unit, and, indeed, all of the remaining material related to the *histoire* recounted in the *discours*, is punctuated with summaries that analeptically explain past events to the reader. These summaries parallel information in the scene/elipse segments. At the same time it is through the use of them that the proleptic announcements of significant actions are introduced at the beginning of the *discours*, and the narrative's final scene is presented. The most notable feature of this arrangement is that both the summaries and elipses devote more and more space, and, thus, time, to shorter or equal periods of the *histoire* as the text progresses. Those portions of the *histoire* that have been shown in preceding sections of this analysis to be vital to the text's structure and development (the card game/chase episodes, and the war and its effects) are the ones most affected by the shifts in durational emphasis. With regard to the effects of the Civil War, the parts of the text devoted to Marré Gamallo best exemplify this process.

This character's first long recollection occupies section II,3 of the text. It is a segment of some twenty-eight pages. While it concentrates on her war-time experience (especially the final days of the conflict and her contact with Luis I. Timoner), it ranges through almost all the propositions of the sequences dealing with her, a period of some forty

120

years.[15] The second insertion referring to her occurs in section IV, 1. A segment of almost the same length (twenty-three pages), it covers virtually the same material, although it does highlight certain elements not as substantially explained in the first occurrence. These include her disillusion during the post-war period, her reasons for returning to Región, and her recollections of the hostage incident during the war.

Her final intervention in the text occupies all of the narrative's penultimate section (IV,3). These nineteen pages deal with a much shorter temporal segment: the period of time during which the war in Región was drawing to a close, and especially how the relationship with Luis I. Timoner affects rest of her life. Here the presentation slows down considerably. Almost as much space as was devoted to forty years is here given over to a relatively short, but crucial period in Marré's life.

A similar process of temporal underscoring is at work in the presentation of the game/chase episodes, particularly as they affect Daniel. The first extended reference to these key events appears during his conversation with Marré in III,1 (pp. 184-185). It recounts the final session of the game, "Una noche de juego en el principio de otoño" (p. 185), and the resultant chase, and its length allows for the inclusion of material that clears up previous briefer references. It also links the figure of María Timoner to the contest for the first time. Later accounts devote more and more space to the incident. The first of these, told by the doctor, occupies the last ten pages of III,1 (pp. 224-233). The total time span of this account is expanded by Daniel's comments to include the entire game (which took over a year) and the chase. While the space dedicated to the description of the final session in the casino is almost identical to the previous one, here the description of the chase is considerably longer, some three pages as opposed to only a few lines in the one before.

15. Towards the close of the text Marré refers to her "cuarentona desazón" (p. 301), which gives a clue to her age.

Directly following this sequence is yet another account of the game, this one provided by the narrator. The account occupies the first twelve pages of III, 2 (pp. 234-245). The bulk of it is devoted to an ancillary component of the game episode —the doctor's involvement with María Timoner— explained in propositions IBC of his series, and IA of the María series. This version, however, devotes more than three times the space to the final action of the card game (pp. 242-245) than did any previous version.

Visible in the preceding examples is a process of dilatation that occurs in the *discours* with respect to the duration of the successive references to important elements of the *histoire*. This process provides a type of spatial or temporal underscoring of the pivotal events by affording them successively expanding treatment in the *discours*. In this manner it serves the emphatic function I mentioned above, in that duration highlights those key elements that were given similar treatment by the order of the *discours*. As such, the duration can be seen to manifest the same type of homological relationship with the world view of the author's collective subject that was perceptible in terms of order.

Frequency also plays a secondary role to order in its relative importance to the structure of the *discours*. The relationship between the occurrence of an event in the *histoire*, and its telling in the *discours*, is singulative in that the *discours* tells n times what happens once in the *histoire*. The continual repetition of fragments of the same action, as has already been demonstrated, keeps that information constantly before the reader. That the repetitions all refer to one singular instance serves to highlight the action of the *histoire* by underscoring uniqueness.

D. Mood

In *Problems of Dostoevsky's Poetics* (Ann Arbor: Ardis, 1973) Mikhail Bakhtin characterizes the Russian novelist's narrative technique as polyphonic in relation to the multiplicity of narrative voices located in his fiction. A similar adjective might well be used to assess the multiplicity of visions or focalizations through which our the reader's visión of the action is filtered, as well as the variety of voices responsible for recounting that action. In fact, this multiplicity, and the manner in which Benet stretches it to its limits, at times leads the reader to believe that the text's narrative system borders on the chaotic. Critical assessments of this aspect of Benetian literary discourse have noted this quality. Some critics have attributed it to Benet's desire to present a Barthian critique at the level of *écriture*.[16] Other relate it to the novelist's decision to obscure the reader's perception of external reality through the text's maze-like structure. Characteristic of this view is Esther Nelson's fine assessment "Narrative Perspective in *Volverás a Región*," *The American Hispanist*, 4, No. 36 (May, 1979), 3-6.

In summary, the fictional universe of *Volverás a Región* is depicted by Daniel Sebastián, Marré Gamallo, a third-person narrator, and the author of the footnotes to the text, which follow the same obscure manner of expression as the other voices. There is no empirical view of the external reality of Región; it is not presented within a neutral context that would allow the reader to gauge the degree to which it is being disfigured by the untrustworthy narrator and the characters who transmit it to us. We hope in vain for objective guideposts within the linguistic tangle, for a source from which we might glean the material we need to judge the accuracy of what lies before us. A sense of layering is produced by the multiplicity of perspectives: that of the implied author who presents the entire verbal space and presumably knows the "truth;" that of the enigmatic "editor," that of the undramatized narrator, those of Marré and Daniel, and finally those voices who speak within the memories of the latter, such as Luis Timoner (pp. 109-111), the doctor's parents-in-law, the miners, and the many anonymous subjects of "dicen que" and "se dicen…" The reader is in the

16. See especially the studies by Gullón and Gimferrer cited previously in this chapter.

presence of a world resembling those elaborate carvings whose concentric spheres can never be perceived simultaneously or in their entirety, but only segmentally, by aligning apertures in the adjacent spheres, and whose innermost layers seem to continue to infinity (pp. 6-7).

To a certain extent I concur with previous studies of this aspect of the narrative's structure. Their limitation lies, in my view, in their failure to perceive the link between this apparent anarchy and the underlying ideological intent of the narrative. A study of narrative transmission in accordance with Genette's categories of mood and voice elucidates this message.

The question of who sees in *Volverás a Region (mode)* offers much less of a problem than the question of who speaks (*voix*). The narrative is centered around three distinct focalizations: that of narrator who knows more than the two characters (*focalisation zéro*, or *non-focalisé* for Genette), and those of the two protagonists of the *discours'* base unit, Marré Gamallo and Daniel Sebastián. Each of them corresponds to category 2B of Genette's assessment of narrative visions: *focalisation interne variable*. The narrative is thus the articulation of three distinct visions. It is through the eyes of the narrator that the entire first chapter (pp. 7-90) is perceived. From the beginning of Chapter II forward, that is to say, from Marré's arrival at the doctor's clinic, and the commencement of their conversation, the one-dimensionality of the single vision is split. The doctor's eyes, as well as those of Marré, begin to probe the events of the past, many of them already hinted at in the non-focused first chapter. The effect is one of a constant shifting of visions, frequently ranging over the same material previously treated from one of the other focalizations. An example of this technique was examined above in another context: the shifting perspective from which the final scene of the card game is recounted in sections III,1 and III,2. The doctor's long description of the action (pp. 224-233) at the close of III,1 is followed in III,2 by a non-focused explanation of the same events, but one that highlights different aspects of them.

Similarly, Marré's second discourse on her wartime experiences and their impact on her concludes section IV,1. As the section closes, she describes her relationship with a young German named Gerd, who is fighting on the side of the Loyalists, and how he became her first lover. "Doctor, en aquel rincón del suelo, bajo aquella manta gris, devoró el alemán mi flor" (p. 281). This account is followed by IV,2, a short non-focused section that treats the final days of the war, and one last Republican attempt to stave off the Nationalist advance. It contains information ancillary to the development of the *histoire* but which parallels the information in Marré's account. Its final sequence describes Gerd's death at the hands of Moorish soldiers, and his brother's attempts to locate the body among the casualties at the edge of a river. "El cadáver se hallaba tendido en la orilla y cubierto de barro, con los pies en el agua. Un perro famélico de color de lana le olfateaba con el hocico entre sus pantalones. El perro gimió, un breve lamento se desvaneció en el vacío glauco del agua y el alba. Lo sacó del agua, lo volvió de cara y lo acostó en la hierba helada" (pp. 292-293).[17] Marré's final verbal intervention in the narrative discourse provides an internaly focused reference to Gerd's death. "Había dejado de temblar pero mis ojos estaban a punto de romper a llorar porque antes de conciliar el sueño le vi muchas veces abandonado en una ribera del río, acribillado a balazos y cubierto de sangre y barro hasta el pecho" (pp. 293-294).

The multiplicity of visions affords a kaleidoscopic or stroboscopic effect to the narrative, offering the reader versions of reality sometimes complementary, as in the examples adduced above, sometimes

17. Typical of the shifting perspectives employed throughout, and Benetian discourse's challenge to the reader in general, is the chronological linkage between these two sections. A close reading of pp. 290-292 indicates that Gerd's death took place on the morning of December 8th. His brother finds him at dawn on the 9th: "Cuando apuntó el alba del día 9" (p. 292). Marré's internally focused account of Gerd's death and its effects on her refers to her inability to sleep after the incident (p. 293), and to a departure sometime during that day. "Creo que aquella misma noche llegamos a El Salvador" (p. 294). Thus the reader is once again forced to backtrack to find out that Marré's account of the incident temporally stands between the account of Gerd's death, and his brother's attempt to find him.

perplexing for their seeming contradictoriness. Illustrative of the latter are the different versions of Daniel's precipitous marriage in the wake of María Timoner's flight: one provided by a long explanatory footnote (pp. 275-276), and another in the body of the text itself (p. 11, p. 257).

Certain anomalies are interposed in this tri-visioned narrative arrangement. Their effect is to create an element of doubt in the text's system of perception.[18] One such instance is the short segment which is focused not on the doctor or Marré, but on Luis I. Timoner (pp. 109-111), in which he comments to Marré on the doctor and his mother. This deviation is significant because it is the only direct intervention of this character in the text other than as the *narrataire* of Marré's long final discourse. His only intervention, however, is not fully his own. At times his sight is heightened by the narrator. This allows Luis to comment on aspects he could not possibly have perceived, such as the doctor's wait for his mother the night they made plans to flee. "La estuvo esperando toda la tarde, con todos los ahorros en el bolsillo, dispuesto a lo que fuera. Lo que había pensado hacer con él lo hizo con mi padre, eso es todo" (p. 110).

Other encroachments of the narrator on the internally focused view of a character involve Daniel Sebastián. A particularly perplexing one is Daniel's description (pp. 202-206) of the card game between the man who will later be Gamallo's opponent in the Región casino, and some of the other men who work with him in the mine. It is difficult enough to imagine the doctor's being able to describe a scene which he did not witness without the narrator's having heightened his perception, but it is virtually impossible for Daniel to reproduce the dialogue that transpired during that night's game without his vision's being meshed with that of the non-focused narrator.

Esther Nelson evoked the image of elaborate carvings to indicate how the multiple perspectives obfuscate an objective perception of the

---

18. These shifting perspectives, as they effect the portrayal of el Numa, are explained in the following chapter.

events that take place in the text. An even more illuminating image would be that of the superimposition of multiple transparencies each containing similar but not identical material, and each pertaining to one of the text's multiple narrative visions. The departure from an "objective" presentation of the textual material does not undermine the narrative discourse to the point of nullifying any assessment of the information contained therein. While it may be difficult to reconstruct the *histoire* from the multiple layers and prespectives of the text, it is not impossible. My analysis up to this juncture demonstrates that fact. The kaleidoscope of narrative foci introduces, then, an element of ambiguity or anarchy into the narrative's verbal structure. This is, however, shrewdly calculated and, rather than block the flow of narrative information transmitted to the reader, impedes it just to a degree that creates doubt. Thus, introduced at the structural level is an element of decay which heightens and complements the ideological message, itself predicated on social decomposition, underlying the text.

E. *Voix*

Volverás a Región is as polyphonic as its vision is kaleidescopic. In almost all cases the message is enunciated by voices that correspond to the eyes through which the action is apprehended; they are those of an unknown narrator, Daniel Sebastián, Marré Gamallo, and several minor figures.[19] There are notable exceptions to the system of voice established in the text. These transgressions are important insofar as they form an integral part of the ideological substratum of the structure of narrative transmission. I will reserve comment on them until I establish the basic structure of this aspect of narrative arrangement in

19. Beginning with Chapter II Benet usually marks the sections of verbal discourse pertaining to Marré and Daniel with quotation marks, while the sections indicating the narrator's speech are left unmarked. Minor narrative voices and those anomalies where one of the characters reports the direct discourse of another, are usually marked with a dash.

order that the significance of these *metalepses*, as Genette calls them, may be clearer. The entire voice system for the text is illustrated in Schematics XI and XII.[20].

Benet's first novel consists of two narrative levels. The voice of the first narrates a text whose narrative instance is *extradiégétique*, or outside the main story line. This voice, in addition, is not a participant in the events he narrates and is therefore *hétérodiégétique*. The first level narration produces a second or *intradiégétique* level. The *temps de la narration* of the primary narrative is *ultérieure*, the narrative act coming after the events. The *temps de la narration* of the second level introduces an interesting situation. In terms of the conversation *in se*, the narrative act is simultaneous to the events being told, but in sense that this dialogue is more than anything else a long series of monologic reconstructions of the past, the narrative act becomes *ultérieure* to the events being recounted.

The first level's narrative instance is located at some undetermined point of time, but one which must be fairly close to the events it recounts. It is directed to an implied *extradiégétique* receptor by a voice who is so aware of the action that takes place at his level and also at the second level of narration, that he displays qualities of super-omniscience that stretch even the classical definition of third-person omniscient narrative employed by Anglo-American point-of-view studies. The familiarity that exists between the narrative voice and the receptor of the text is seen in the text's opening lines. The narrator begins his discourse in the following manner: "Es cierto, el viajero que saliendo de Región pretende llegar a su sierra..." (p. 7). As Ricardo Gullón astutely remarks in his *Insula* article, it appears as if the narrator begins in response to a question by the *narrataire*. "Literalmente la novela no comienza; su principio es una continuación, una respuesta a algo que ya se dijo o se pensó" (p. 10). The narrator's interventions in the text, then, seem to be part of a dialogue with the *narrataire* in which

---

20. Minor narrative voices include those of Luis I. Timoner and the disturbed child, both of whose direct interventions in the narrative are limited.

the real reader "overhears" only that portion uttered by the former. In this way a certain structural parallel is established with the incomplete dialogue that characterizes the second level of narration. While both the voices and the receptos at that level are within the system (*intradiégétique*), the monologue-like character of this interchange provides the same incompleteness as does the emitter/receptor structure at the first level. There the reader is given only half of the communicative system. At the second level both halves are provided, but less communication between narrator and receiver takes place: the doctor and Marré seem, at best, only marginally interested in what the other has to say.

The familiarity with which the narrator addresses the *narrataire* is emphasized at subsequent junctures in the text. For instance I,2 begins "En aquella ocasión no se trataba de una vieja camioneta..." (p. 15). This once more seems to imply that the reader has interrupted the narrator's discourse at an instant in which he once again begins a response to the *narrataire*. Indicative of this is the use of "en aquella ocasión" as a way of beginning, implying that the other occasions have already been mentioned. The first lines of I,5 ("así, pues, el viajero que partiendo de Macerta..." (p. 51)), phrased very much like the start of I,1, give the same impression.[21]

The narrator's acquaintance with the text's action, its characters, and with their own second level verbal discourse is another essential property demonstrated throughout. Section II,2, for example, commences as follows:

21. It is this proximity between the *narrataire* and the narrator that is responsible for much of the confusion that the reader experiences proceeding through the text. The system is so difficult to penetrate that opening lines like "en aquella ocasión no se trataba de una vieja camioneta" with their implicit communicativeness for the *narrataire*, leave the real reader perplexed and confused since, as was demonstrated above, the antecedent information needed to process such statements at the time they are emitted has not been provided.

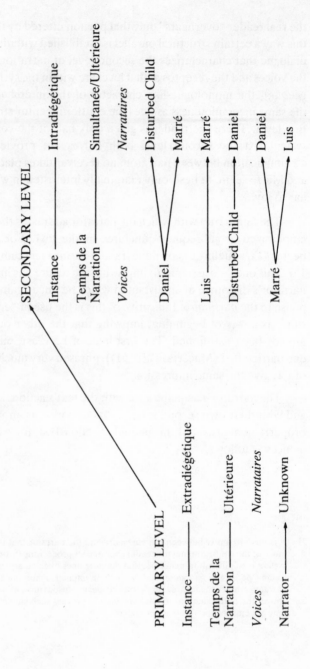

**Schematic XI
System
of
Narrative Transmission**

PRIMARY LEVEL

Instance —— Extradiégétique

Temps de la
Narration —— Ultérieure

Voices — *Narrataires*

Narrator —▸ Unknown

SECONDARY LEVEL

Instance —— Intradiégétique

Temps de la
Narration —— Simultanée/Ultérieure

Voices — *Narrataires*

Daniel —▸ Disturbed Child

Luis —▸ Marré

Disturbed Child —▸ Marré

Marré —▸ Daniel

—▸ Daniel

—▸ Luis

130

Schematic XII
Relationship Narrator/Account
&
Narrator/Narrative Level

Level Relationship	EXTRADIEGETIQUE	INTRADIEGETIQUE
	NARRATOR	
HETERODIEGETIQUE		
HOMODIEGETIQUE		MARRE GAMALLO DANIEL SEBASTIAN LUIS I. TIMONER DISTURBED CHILD

"Porque la casa" —le había de decir el doctor mientras observaba la lluvia, a través de la ventana del despacho, con las manos cruzadas a la espalda; por fin había dejado el maletín y se había echado el abrigo sobre los hombros, con el cuello alzado. Había amainado la intensidad de la tormenta; un gorrión posado en el antepecho de la ventana se sacudía las gotas de las alas y, con bruscos movimientos de su cabeza, estudiaba los árboles del otro lado de la carretera para elegir uno donde pasar la noche; en lo alto de aquellos chopos comenzaron a oírse los últimos gorjeos de sus compañeros que, ocultos entre el follaje, le anunciaban el fin de la lluvia. Pasó el dedo por el canto del marco de la ventana y observó la huella de polvo que había dejado sobre la yema —"fue una de esas compras tardías que cuestan cinco o diez mil veces más que el dinero entregado al antiguo propietario si todo lo que cuesta a partir del momento en que se reciben el título y las llaves pudiera medirse en dinero (p. 120).

The *extradiégétique* narrative voice here interrupts the second level discourse in mid-sentence to intercalate background information, thus manifesting the degree of its omniscience, and the proximity of the narrative instance of the first level to the action of the second. Similarly, III,2 begins as follows:

El doctor se había percibido de un cambio; no sólo la encontraba más distante, no sólo aceptaba su compañía no con el desenfado de antes sino con la resignación que impone toda exclusión, sino que toda su actitud para con la gente que la rodeaba y admiraba parecía dañida de una reserva que —el Doctor lo sabía muy bien— no se podía atribuir solamente al cansancio o a la timidez. Desde el primer día en que se puso en juego la sortija el Doctor comprendió que por parte de ella —y de manera tácita, por tanto mucho más irremediable— había quedado roto uno de los vínculos que le unía a su amante (p. 234).

As was demonstrated earlier, the last pages of III,1 describe the final scene of the card game, and Gamallo's maiming as seen and recounted by Daniel Sebastián. The narrator starts the next section by introducing relevent background information pertinent to the doctor's participation in the game that was not included in Sebastián's narrative. This voice also makes qualitative judgments about Sebastián's action. The first of these is set off parenthetically through the use of dashes: "—el Doctor lo sabía muy bien." Later on the omniscient narrator's voice not only qualifies the doctor's thoughts but also judges María's intentions parenthetically within the same sentence: "Desde el primer día en que se puso en juego la sortija el Doctor comprendió que por parte de ella —y de manera tácita, por tanto mucho más irremediable—."

Another striking example of both the omniscience of the first level narrator and his verbal intrusion on the *intradiégétique* narration occurs at the juncture of sections III,2 and III,3. Daniel Sebastián's previously described narrative in the former ends with a sentence fragment. "Y, todavía le diré otra cosa..." (p. 254). The narrator's first sentence in the next section finishes the doctor's utterance. "Pero no le dijo cómo aquella tarde a finales de septiembre había perdido a María Timoner" (p. 255). Here once again the *extradiégétique* voice provides information omitted by Daniel.

The transition between IV,1 and IV,2, a juncture examined above for the aspects of mood that it elucidated, is yet another illustration of the process I have been discussing. Marré ends her account of her wartime experiences with a reference to her attempt to sleep while a nighttime battle raged nearby. "Enfrente de nosotros, y no muy lejos, la hoya del río quedaba iluminada por el resplandor del combate cuyo fragor nos acompañó durante aquel difícil sueño" (p. 285). The following section begins with the *extradiégétique* voice explaining exactly which battle Marré had in mind in her last sentence, and does so in a comment syntactically linked to her words: "Se trataba del combate que la primera decena de noviembre..." (p. 285).

The narrative instance of the second or *intradiégétique* level is the time span encompassed by the base sequence of the *discours*. Its primary voices are Marré Gamallo and Daniel Sebastián, with short interventions by both the disturbed child and Luis I. Timoner.

All the *intradiégétique* voices are *homodiégétique* since they participate in the action they recount. The receptors, as Genette prescribes for a second degree system, are also *intradiégétique*. The *narrataire* for Luis' short intervention is Marré. Her narrative segments are directed at Luis, in the brief sections beginning on p. 307, and, for the rest of the time at Daniel Sebastián. The doctor's entire discourse, except for the few words he speaks to the disturbed child (pp. 92, 97, 98, 314), is directed to Marré. The child's few utterances are directed to Daniel.

Important transgressions of the system sketched above occur in several crucial areas: the shifting omniscience of the *extradiégétique* narrator, the occurrences of voice heightening for Marré and Daniel Sebastián, and the footnotes inserted in the text. At various moments in the narrative discourse, the narrator's extremely omniscient voice appears somewhat tentative. In III,1 he interrupts the doctor's discourse to comment on it parenthetically. "'Yo creo que por aquel tiempo' —había de añadir el Doctor, y si no lo añadió lo pudo hacer— 'también se inventó el verano'" (p. 216). While the narrative voice is once again aware enough of the second level discourse to be able to comment on it, here the commentator's information is less certain: he is not sure exactly what the doctor said, adding an element of doubt to his knowledge, a quality not visible in examples studied earlier.

Several instances appear in which the *extradiégétique* voice's account of the events seems to precede, rather than follow the actions it recounts. As Marré Gamallo arrives at Daniel's clinic, the text includes within the narrator's account a segment of the doctor's speech. This passage, in turn, contains a brief interpolation by the narrator. "Ah, no es el tiempo —dirá después, cuando abra la puerta— ni siquiera el miedo, el único aparato de medida que tiene la conciencia; es la falta de otra cosa lo que le hace ser algo. Es la falta de otra cosa..." (p. 95). The narrator's use of the future tense indicates that he is anticipating not only the doctor's action (opening the door), but also what Daniel will utter at that instant, transgressing in this manner the temporal axis of the first level narrative by shifting from an *ultérieure* to an *anterieure temps de la narration*, and modulating his own voice by bringing it close to the doctor's words. An almost identical transgression of the system occurs in III,1. "'El acto tercero —o el que sea— se refiere a las desventuras del escuadrón', dirá el Doctor más adelante, 'desde los primeros momentos de su formación en torno a la mesa de juego donde hemos dejado...'" (p. 244). Once again the narrator interrupts the account to explain what Daniel will say at a later juncture of the text. This provides another example of the narrator's sliding from his normally *ultérieure* position to one which anticipates the action.

Another type of transgression is found when one of the *intradiégétique* voices is heightened by the *extradiégétique* one, producing an overlapping of the two levels. The account in the mood section of how the narrator sharpens Luis' sight is equally indicative of the same process with regard to voice. This aspect is particularly noticeable in Timoner's use of phrases habitually employed by the narrator, such as "es cierto" (p. 109, p. 110). It is also perceptible in syntax, especially when Luis employs a complex sentence starting with a dependent clause whose first words are "asi que" (p. 110). The process is again discernable at the begining of III,1, only this time it is the voice of Daniel Sebastián who adopts the narrator's syntactic habits. There the doctor starts his discourse with a slight variant of the "it is certain" construction used repeatedly by the *extradiégétique* voice. "No sé si sería cierto pero tenía muy buenas razones para decirlo..." (p. 180).

An extended example of the doctor's voice being meshed with the narrator's is provided by the former's long description of the geo-climatic coordinates of the area which virtually parallels, element for element, the narrator's even longer account in I,1 (pp. 27-53). One striking illustration is Sebastián's description of the problems encountered by travellers who attempt to reach Región's mountain. "Al viajero inadvertido que trate de llegar al corazón de la serranía —o que aspire a escalar la cumbre del Monje..." (p. 210). As will be recalled, very similar phrasing is employed by the narrator in I,1 (p. 7), and I,5 (p. 5).

Another aspect of voice heightening involves instances where the doctor's voice is raised to such an extent that he can report the speech of other characters, sometimes in a situation he witnessed, other times on occasions at which he was not present. An example of the latter was examined above in my discussion of mood: Daniel's reporting the speech of the miners during their card game (pp. 204-206). The numerous occasions on which Sebastián reproduces the speech acts of Gamallo and his opponet during the card game (pp. 226-229, 230-231) are additional examples of this super-imposition of narrative levels.

The several footnotes that are appended to the body of the text also represent transgressions of the system of narrative transmission. In "Narrative Perspective..." Esther Nelson attributes the notes to another voice —an "editor" is the term she employs— because the information contained in them at times contradicts accounts provided in the body of the text. The most obvious example of this is the differing account of Daniel's marriage noted in my analysis of mood. I prefer, nevertheless, to attribute these notes, which appear on pp. 20, 109, 275-77, 312, to the *extradiégétique* voice, and to treat the contradictory information contained in them as yet another exceptional means by which the system is transgressed.

Mood and voice control the flow of information received by the reader, and the quality of that data. In *Volverás a Región*, both characteristics inherent in the system and transgressions of those norms serve to emphasize the ideological message underlying the text. The closed nature of the emiter/receptor circuit introduces within the system an implied difficulty for the real reader. Rather than fostering communication, the system, in essence, breaks down, thereby increasing the reader's confusion. This is mirrored in the *intradiégétique* narrative where the breakdown becomes a feature of the non-communicative relationship between that level's two primary narrative voices.

The very multiplicity of voices and perspectives reflects the same type of structural fragmentation seen in my analysis of the temporal aspects of the *discour*'s structure. This multiplicity provides a first step toward a possible deterioration that is actualized in the text through the many transgressions of the system The transmitting structure, then, contains elements that put into question or erode the stability of the total structure. Far from causing a breakdown in meaning, as some critics have asserted, the structure of the text's presentation of *mode* and *voix* provide a clear structural homology with the anti-regime collective subject. Just as the latter posits decay and decadence as the result of francoism, so does the structural fabric of *mode* and *voix* imbue narrative structure with the same corruptive force. The attack at the level of *écriture* is certainly here. Seen in the light of the critical model employed in this essay, however, it provides a key that strengthens the message underlying the text.

As was the case with the text's *histoire*, the analysis of its *discours*, by pointing out the meaning-bearing elements of the text's syntactical disposition, reveals that behind the seemingly indecipherable temporal aspects of order stands a structural message that parallels and emphasizes that of the *histoire*. This message is underscored by the less important categories of duration and frequency, which, nonetheless serve an emphatic function. The narrative transmission of the information analyzed under *temps* is further strengthened by the way in which the implicit decay of the narrative's structure underscores the homological relationship with the anti-regime collective subject. Thus all the major aspects of the narrative discourse's structure demonstrate that behind the content of the text lies a structural disposition that articulates an ideological stance critical of the francoist regime.

CHAPTER IV*

Juan Benet's Intertextual Web

*   A shorter verson of this chapter was read at the Mountain Interstate Foreign Language Conference in October, 1976. After this study was completed Professor Robert Spires published "*Volverás a Región* y la desintegración total," in his *La novela española de postguerra* (Barcelona: CUPSA, 1978), pp. 224-246, which also explores aspects of the Benet/Frazer link. As our goals are different, and our methodologies diverse, this excellent essay does not substantially alter the findings of my study.

     Benet published "Una leyenda: Numa," in his *Del pozo y del numa: Un ensayo y una leyenda* (Barcelona: La Gaya Ciencia, 1978), pp. 96-168. His discussion elaborates on the personage of el Numa, but is not of importance for this study since the link I wish to establish is between two specific texts: Frazer's *The Golden Bough*, and Benet's first novel. It remains for another to investigate how the information contained in this fictional discourse may modify the picture of the guardian of the forest of Mantua that I have presented.

I
Introduction

This chapter examines how the intertextual connection between *Volverás a Región* and elements of Sir James Frazer's exposition in his classic *The Golden Bough* reinforces the ideological message that informs the novel's structure. Specifically it explores Benet's construction of his enigmatic el Numa, one of the key personages in his text, who apparently has qualities borrowed directly from Frazer's discussion of the King of the Wood, guardian of the sacred grove at Nemi. The manner in which the Spanish writer alters Frazer's explanation to fit his needs will form the central part of my discussion. But I will also touch on how the novelist injects material based on *The Golden Bough* into his creation of the text's narrative space.[1]

The recognition of this process is linked to the reader's literary competence. Once aware of the structural parallels between the two works, one can perceive that Benet has inverted the meaning of many of the elements modeled on Frazer, and that the nature of the textual dialogue hinges on the effect created by that inversion. This ironic reversal permits Benet to exploit the link between the two works in such a way as to cast greater light on the ideological message inherent in the syntagmatic organization of *histoire* and *discours*.

---

1. My decision to concentrate on the intertextual dialogue between *The Golden Bough* and *Volverás a Región* to the exclusion of other works that intertextually nourish Benet's novel was motivated by the belief that the dialogue between Benet and Frazer is the most important of the threads in the intertextual web that Benet weaves, and the one that bears most directly on the work's underlying ideology.

This chapter is divided into two sections. The first delineates those elements of *The Golden Bough* pertinent to the comprehension of Benet's manipulation of their meaning. The second analyzes how Benet structures this dialogue.

My intention here is not to write either myth criticism as it has generally come to be construed, or an influence study as practiced by comparatists. The former has as its goal the isolation of factors in a work that disclose its universal character. It moves from the particular text to the universal myth or archetype that is perceived to be underlying it.[2] What is of interest to me, rather, is the way Benet has chosen one of the classics of anthropology and used it to fit his needs. Additionally, Sir James' influence is the given with which this chapter begins. Benet acknowledges Frazer in his essay "Breve historia de *Volverás a Región*," which describes the creative process involved in writing his text.

Aún cuando en la última página de este libro señala que fue escrito entre 1962-1964, entre Madrid y el Pantano de Porma en la Provincia de León, la historia y los orígenes distan de ser tan simples y se remontan a algunos años atrás. Lo cierto es que hacia 1951, bajo el influjo sufrido por la lectura de *La rama dorada*, comencé a escribir una novela —que terminaría un par de años después— en la que se narraban unos cuantos acontecimientos situados en un mismo medio rural (que a falta de una precisa localización bauticé con el nombre de Región) dominado por la lejana nocturna y omnipo-

---

2. The widely used primer in literary criticism *A Handbook of Critical Approaches to Literature*, written by Wilfred L. Guerin *et al* (New York: Harper and Row, 1966), in one of the several chapters that is dedicated to myth and archetypal criticism, characterizes the goal of myth criticism in the following manner. "The Myth critic is concerned to seek out those mysterious artifacts built into certain literary 'forms' which elicit, with almost uncanny force, dramatic and universal reactions. He wishes to discover how it is that certain works of literature, usually those that have become, or promise to become 'classics,' imagine a kind of reality to which readers give perennial response —while other works, seemingly as well constructed, and even some forms of reality, leave us cold" (p. 216).

tente presencia del guarda de una finca, una suerte de vicario en nuestras tierras del guardián del bosque sagrado de Nemi.[3]

Thus my primary intent here is to explore how Benet structures a specific intertextual dialogue, and the implications of this modeling process for his novel's meaning.

3. Juan Benet, "Breve historia de *Volverás a Región,*" *Revista de Occidente*, NS 134 (May 1976), p. 160. This also serves as the prologue to the second edition of the novel (Madrid: Alianza Editorial, 1974). The author's recent "La historia editorial y judicial de *Volverás a Región,*" published in his most recent collection of essays *La moviola de Eurípides* (Madrid: Taurus, 1981), pp. 31-44, explains the complicated reasons behind the withdrawal of the Alianza Editorial edition.

II
Sir James Frazer and *The Golden Bough*

The Golden Bough is one of those classics that has exercised a wide-ranging influence, not only on its own discipline, but on the intellectual development of the twentieth century as a whole. As one of the pioneer explorations that helped to shape comparative studies of mankind, its importance to anthropology and folklore is immense. Studies have also documented its influence on other disciplines, and particularly on the thought of such important figures as Freud, Jung, Spengler, Bergson, and Cassirer.[4] As the distinguished scholar Theodor H. Gaster has stated in the introduction to his abridgement of *The Golden Bough*: "It can be said without reasonable fear of contradiction that no other work in the field of anthropology has contributed so much to the mental and artistic climate of our times. Indeed, what Freud did for the individual, Frazer did for civilization as a whole" (p. xix).[5]

---

4. Chapter III of John B. Vickery's important study, *The Literary Impact of the Golden Bough* (Princeton: Princeton University Press, 1973), entitled "The Intellectual Influence of *The Golden Bough,*" deals extensively with Frazer's impact on the major thinkers of this century.
   21

5. *The Golden Bough*, edited with notes and forward by Theodor H. Gaster (New York: Mentor Books, 1964). All quotations from Gaster's forward are taken from this edition.
   The history of the editions of *The Golden Bough* is somewhat involved. It was first published in two volumes in 1890. Over a period of years Frazer expanded it to twelve, and then added a thirteenth entitled *Aftermath*. He then wrote a one-volume abridged version. All citations in this chapter are taken from the abridged version (New York: Macmillan, 1963).

The very number and stature of writers who have fallen under Frazer's influence is impressive.[6] The most conspicuous example is perhaps T. S. Eliot in *The Waste Land,* but Frazer's presence can also be felt in Joyce, Lawrence, Mann, and Graves. The work's influence on literary criticism is perhaps even more noteworthy since it is one of the works that has provided the theoretical basis for mythological and archetypal interpretations of literature.

Juan Benet is thus in good company when he utilizes Frazer's book as a source. Perhaps the best way to elucidate the manner in which Benet handles Frazer is to begin with a brief overview of *The Golden Bough*'s underlying ideas and structure. I will also point out elements of Frazer's work that while not central to his thesis are tied to his discussion of the King of the Wood, since it is this figure that contributes most to an understanding of Benet's adaptation.

The work begins with Frazer's evocation of Turner's pictoral rendition of the Golden Bough:

Who does not know Turner's picture of the Golden Bough? The scene, suffused with the golden glow of imagination in which the divine mind of Turner steeped and transfigured even the fairest natural landscape, is a dream -like vision of the little woodland lake of Nemi- "Diana's Mirror," as it was called by the ancients. No one who has seen the calm water, lapped in a green hollow of the Alban hills, can ever forget it. The two characteristic Italian villages which

There remains another problem bearing on the editions of *The Golden Bough*: what edition did Benet read? Since his knowledge of English has been amply demonstrated, it would not be surprising that he would have read either the long or the short version in their original language. There does exist one Spanish translation of the one-volume edition of *The Golden Bough* done in the 1940's in Mexico by Fondo de Cultura Económica. According to Professor Miguel Enguídanos, who studied anthropology in Spain, the Spanish translation was widely read and circulated in university circles precisely during the period in which Benet states, in "Breve historia de *Volverás a Región*," that he fell under the influence of Sir James' classic. I therefore assume that Benet read a one-volume edition of the work, either in English or in Spanish.

6. See Vickery's study for a detailed analysis of Frazer's influence on both major and minor authors alike.

slumber on its banks, and the equally Italian palace whose terraced gardens descend steeply to the lake, hardly break the stillness and even the solitariness of the scene. Diana herself might still linger by this lonely shore, still haunt these woodlands wild (p. 7).

Into this description of sylvan landscape and calm water, on whose northern shore once stood the sacred grove and sanctuary of Diana Nemorosis (Diana of the Wood), which was also known as the lake and grove of Aricia, Frazer projects the image of a grim figure, the protagonist of what he himself describes as "...a strange and recurring tragedy" (p. 1).

In this sacred grove grew a certain tree round which at any time of the day, and probably far into the night, a grim figure might be seen to prowl. In his hand he carried a drawn sword, and he kept peering warily about him as if at every instant he expected to be set upon by an enemy. He was a priest and a murderer; and the man for whom he looked was sooner or later to murder him and hold the priesthood in his stead. Such was the rule of the sanctuary. A candidate for the priesthood could only succeed to office by slaying the priest, and having slain him, he retained office till he was himself slain by a stronger or a craftier.

The post which he held by this precarious tenure carried with it the title of king; but surely no crowned head ever lay uneasier, or was visited by more evil dreams than this. For year in, year out, in summer and winter, in fair weather and foul, he had to keep his lonely watch, and whenever he snatched a troubled slumber it was at the peril of his life. The least relaxation of his vigilance, the smallest abatement of his strength of limb or skill of force, put him in jeopardy; grey hairs might seal his death-warrant. To the gentle and pious pilgrims at the shrine the sight of him might well seem to darken the fair landscape, as when a cloud suddenly blots the sun on a bright day. The dreamy blue Italian skies, the dapple shade of summer woods, the sparkle of waves in the sun, can have accorded but ill with that stern and sinister figure. Rather we picture ourselves the scene as it may have been witnessed by a belated wayfarer on one of those wild autumn nights when the dead leaves are falling thick and the winds seem to sing the dirge of the dying year. It is a somber picture, set to melancholy music—the background of forest showing black and jagged against a lowering and stormy sky, the sighing of the wind in the branches, the rustle of the withered leaves underfoot, the lapping of the cold water on the shore, and in the foreground pacing to and fro, now in twilight, and now in gloom a dark figure with a glitter of steel at the shoulder whenever the pale moon, riding clear of the cloudrack, peers down at him through the matted bough (pp. 1-2).

The figure so described, and condemned to wander endlessly in fear of his life, is the King of the Wood. Unable to find any precedent in classical antiquity for either the rite or the figure, Frazer proposes to look elsewhere in hopes of finding an explanation. "Accordingly, if we can show that a barbarous custom, like the priesthood at Nemi, has existed elsewhere; if we can detect the motives which led to its institution; if we can prove that these motives have operated widely, perhaps universally, in human society, producing in varied circumstances a variety of institutions specifically different, but generically alike, if we can show lastly, that these varied motives, with some of their derivative institutions, were actually at work in classical antiquity; then we may fairly infer that at a remoter age the same motives gave birth to the priesthood at Nemi" (p. 2). *The Golden Bough* is Frazer's attempt to do just that, to "...offer a fairly probable explanation of the priesthood at Nemi" (p. 3).

Frazer sets down two questions that must be answered in order to solve the riddle of the rite at Nemi. "First, why had Diana's priest at Nemi, the King of the Wood, to slay his predecessor? Second, why before doing so had he to pluck the branch of a certain tree which the public opinion of the ancients identified with Virgil's Golden Bough?" (p. 10).

His quest for the answer to the two questions that would explain the rite led him far and wide, only to return to eventually Nemi in the book's last section. What Frazer was able to demonstrate through his analysis and presentation of an overwhelming amount of material were the similarities of practices in primitive societies spread throughout the world, and, just as importantly, their survival, now for the most part devoid of their original character, in customs practiced in more advanced societies. As Gaster phrases it, "for as Freud deepened men's insight into the behavior of individuals by uncovering the ruder world of the subconscious, from which so much of it springs, so Frazer enlarged man's understanding of the behavior of societies by laying bare the primitive concepts and modes of thought which underlie and inform many of their institutions and which persist, as a subliminal element in their culture, in their traditional folk customs" (pp. xx).

The King of the Wood, and the rite that governed his comportment in Diana's grove at Nemi, are thus seen as prototypical of the nature of kingship in primitive societies.[7] He is prototype of the god-king as found in those societies. Partaking of magical powers due to his divine nature, he is at the same time priest and king, god and man. Because of his divine nature and his magical powers his people identified his personal existence with the life cycle of nature and of themselves. They felt themselves sympathetically bound up to him, and per-

---

7. Somewhat ironically, what for Sir James was the major thread of his study, namely, the nature of the rite at the Arician grove, has been proven erroneous by later scholarship. As Gaster points out in his forward:

    Frazer's interpretation of the priesthood of Aricia, and of the rites which governed succession to it has been almost unanimously rejected by classical scholars. The sanctuary at that place was probably no more than an asylum for runaway slaves; and the golden bough, far from being a vessel of divine power or identical with that carried by Aeneas his journey to the nether world, was in all likelihood simply the branch characteriscally borne in antiquity by suppliants at a shrine. Accordingly, Frazer's elaborate exposition of primitive customs and their modern survivals must now be read as a treatise in its own right, and not as an illustrative commentary on the ancient Latin institutions. (Since, however, it is impossible to eliminate all references to the latter without destroying the whole structure of the book, it has seemed best to retain it with this express warning that it must now be regarded only as an artistic and fanciful *leitmotif*, not as a factual scaffolding and that the title *The Golden Bough*, is in truth a misnomer) (p. xvi).

ceived in his physical condition the key to their survival or their perishing. To assure the well-being of the community, it was necessary to protect the king from harm. To this end an elaborate system of taboos was set up to maintain the safety of both the ruler and the ruled. Moreover it was vitally necessary that the king be replaced at the slightest indication of the deterioration of his physical condition, lest this decay lead to the blight and destruction of his subjects and their crops.[8] The only way to insure against the waning of the king's powers was to put him to death at the least sign of the weakening of his physical condition. Later this was in some societies regularized in the custom of putting him to death at regular intervals. In more advanced cultures this actual killing of the king was replaced by surrogate figures' taking the place of the king, or with a purely symbolic rather than a literal death.

The manner of perceiving kingship in primitive societies accounts for the King of the Wood's having to be slain and replaced with someone who has proven himself stronger through combat, in an ever-recurring cycle bent on protectiong the well-being of the subjects sympathetically bound to him. While accidentally slightly different (the King of the Wood at least enjoyed the opportunity to meet his challenger in combat), the ritual at Nemi is essentially the same one that

8. Vickery points out the link between taboos and the sympathetic relationship between the king and his people.

    The [king's] life is protected by a system of precautions or safeguards still more numerous and minute than those which in primitive societies every man adopts for the safety of his own soul. Their general effect is to isolate the king and so to limit his accessibility, particularly for strangers. The taboos which regulate the life of the priest-king are imposed upon him by his people rather than demanded by him out of an obsessive regard for his own welfare. The minute rules of taboo that regulate his life aim at preserving the established order of nature and avoiding the destruction of the world, which which is thought to eventuate from the natural death of the king. To many primitive peoples, we must remember, the priest-king is regarded as the incarnation of various divine beings, that is, he constitutes the connnecting link between men and the gods. From the latter stems all power and potency wielded by men, hence, it is essential that the link be preserved unbroken. Since the king is both man and god, he of all men is more intimately in contact with the power of life. As a result, his life is considered to be sympathetically bound up with the prosperity and welfare of the country as a whole (pp. 49-50).

Frazer finds underlying the nature of kingship as practiced in primitive societies in general.[9]

Central to this conception of kingship is its cyclical nature. Frazer himself, in the quotation drawn from the first page of his work, refers to the rite at Nemi as *recurring* tragedy. This idea of death for the sake of rebirth is central to Frazer's thesis. It regulates the life cycle of the people just as it regulates the cycle of natural phenomena upon which the people depend.

Deriving from the concept of the killing of the divine king is the idea of the scapegoat. This notion is based on the belief that by transferring the corruptions of the tribe to a sacred animal or individual, and then by killing, and, in some cases eating, this scapegoat, the group would be able to atone, and insure its natural and spiritual rebirth.

Thus in his search for an explanation to the first of his two main questions, Frazer bared the essential similarity of man's comportment. The answer to the second question is also found far from Nemi. Although not as central as the first question, it too reveals this similarity. Frazer shows that the Golden Bough, the branch that the King of the Wood's successor had to pluck before attempting to kill him, is the mistletoe, and that the tree on which it grows is the oak, associated in classical mythology with Jupiter as god of thunder. The key element in his proof is the relationship between the Norse god Balder, himself an oak deity, and the mistletoe. Frazer shows the link between the mistletoe and Balder's death, and points out that the life of the god is seen to be tied to the life of the mistletoe, just as the life of the oak is seen to be tied to the life of the mistletoe that parasitically grows on it.[10]

9. A modification of this is detectable in the habit of simple combat practiced by the King of the Wood at Nemi. It still constitutes a check on his physical condition, but it also affords him a kind of temporary reprieve not originally available (Vickery, p. 51).

10. The idea that the life of the oak was in the mistletoe was probably suggested, as I have said, by the observation that in winter the mistletoe growing on the oak remains green while the oak itself is leafless. But the position of the plant —growing

Since for Frazer the Golden Bough is the mistletoe, it is understandable that the person wishing to succeed the King of the Wood should be required to pluck it and thus symbolically reduce the strength of the one he wished to kill. This also explains why the touching of the mistletoe by any other person was a tabooed act in the grove at Nemi (p. 815). Frazer returned to Nemi after having ventured far afield to solve the riddle of the rite at the Arician grove.[11] We must do the same to delineate the information that the author of *The Golden Bough* presents about the relationship of the King of the Wood to the other figures found in the Arician grove. This is necessary since it comes into play in Benet's reforging of the character of the King of the Wood in *Volverás a Región*.

There are in fact two parallel sets of characters important to the rite at Diana's temple whose lives are intertwined. The first of these sets consists of the King of the Wood and the goddess Diana. According to Frazer the mythological origins of the priest at Diana's temple, and of the temple itself, are to be found in the fate of the young Greek hero Hippolytus, who was said to have passed his days in the forests with the virgin Greek goddess Artemis, the Greek counterpart of Diana, as his only companion. Proud of his relationship with the goddess, he spurns the love of women. Aphrodite, wounded by his coldness toward her, seeks revenge that eventually leads to the youth's death. However, Diana saves him and bears him away to the grove at Nemi, where she entrusts him to the water nymph Egeria. Here he lived unknown under the name of Virbius, reigned as king, and dedicated a part of the grove to a temple for the goddess who had saved him.

For Frazer, Virbius is the mythological predecessor of the line of priests who served Diana at her temple in the Arician grove, who, as

not from the ground but from the trunk or branches of the tree— might confirm this idea (Frazer, p. 813).

11. In Chapter IV of his study, entitled "Impact and Archetype," Vickery points out that the structure of *The Golden Bough* itself is that of a quest romance. It cyclically bends back to where it starts, the grove at Nemi, after the nature of the riddle that the author sought to solve has been resolved.

has been noted, were known by the title of the King of the Wood. "In the character of the founder of the sacred grove and the first king of Nemi, Virbius is clearly the mythical predecessor or archetype of the first of a line of priests who served Diana under the title of Kings of the Wood, and who came, like him, one after the other, to a violent end" (p. 9). He then proceeds to demonstrate that the priests who served Diana at her temple stood in the same relationship to her as did Virbius: that is to say they too were husbands of the goddess. In addtion, since Diana, in her widest acceptance is, a symbol of fertility, she herself must be fertile. Hence the importance of the marriage between the King of the Wood and Diana which is seen as a way of promoting fertility of the earth.

This relationship between Diana and the King of the Wood was paralleled in the Arician grove by the one between the water nymph Egeria and the wise King Numa.[12] According to tradition, Egeria had been the king's wife or mistress, and had consorted with him in the secrecy of the sacred grove. The laws which, according to legends, Numa gave to the Romans are supposed to have resulted from his inspiration by Egeria's divinity. Since Egeria is perhaps only another form of the nature goddess Diana, Frazer sees the relationship bet-

---

12. *The Encyclopedia Britannica* (15th ed., 1974), under the heading Numa Pompilius, gives the following information about this Roman king:
    ...second of the seven kings, who, according to Roman tradition ruled the Republic (c. 509 BC). He is said to have reigned from 715 to 673. Numa is credited with the formulation of the religious calendar, and with the founding of nearly all the earliest religious institutions, including the Vestal Virgins, the cults of Mars, Jupiter, and Romulus (quirinus); and the office of *pontifex maximus*. These develments were, however, undoubtedly the result of centuries of religious accretion, going back to prehistoric times and continuing down to the republic era, and thus not to be assigned to any single man...
    ...According to legend, Numa is the peaceful counterpart of the more bellicose Romulus, the mythical founder of Rome, whom he succeeded after an interregnum of one year. His supposed relationship with Pythagoras was chronologically impossible, and the 14 books relating to philosophy and religious (pontifical) law that were uncovered in 181 BC are clearly forgeries.
    Similar information is provided by Michael Grant's and John Hazel's recent work *Gods and Mortals in Classical Mythology* (Springfield, Mass.: G & C Merriam, 1976) under the heading Numa Pompilius.
    23

ween Numa and Egeria as a duplication of the one described above between Diana and the King of the Wood.

The convergence of the two distinct lines of inquiry suggests that the legendary union of the Roman king with Egeria may have been a reflection or duplicate of the union of the King of the Wood with Egeria or her double Diana. This does not imply that the Roman kings ever served as King of the Wood in the Arician grove, but only that that they may originally have hald office on similar terms. To be more explicit, it may been invested with a sacred character of the same kind, and may be possible that they reigned, not by right of birth, but in virtue of their supposed divinity as representatives or embodiments of a god, and that as such they mated with a goddess, and had to prove their fitness from time to time to discharge their divine functions by engaging in a severe bodily struggle which often may have proved fatal to them, leaving the crown to their victorious adversary (pp. 170-171).

This far from exhausts the information Frazer affords us about these two sets of relationships. The rest of the facts show that the two parallel or duplicate sets of characters are related to each other

---

The mythical second king of Rome, invited to succeed Romulus: according to tradition he reigned from 715 to 673 BC. He was said to be of Sabine origin, and it was for his piety that the Romans asked him to rule them. They attributed to him the foundation and formulation of most of their religious rituals, including the worship of Janus: he was believed to have established the college of Vestal Virgins. It was thought that his mistress, the water-goddess Egeria, who lived in a grove near the Capena gate, gave Numa much instruction in religious and legal matters. When his wife Tatis died, Numa married the nymph. Numa was contrasted in the Roman mind with Romulus, for he was as peaceful as his predecessor had been warlike. Later writers sometimes said that Numa learned his wisdom from the Greek philosopher Pythagoras (who, in fact, for all his legendary aspects was an historical figure, and lived long after Numa's traditional epoch). This may be explained by the strength of Pythagorean mysticism in Southern Italy.

In a recent interview with Nelson Orringer published in *Los ensayistas*, Nos. 8-9 (March 1980), pp. 59-65, Benet discusses his favorite Greek and Roman writers. Among them is Plutarch, and it is entirely possible that the latter's treatment of Numa Pompilius was another source for Benet's figure that needs further exploration.

through their common link to the god Jupiter, the supreme God of the Romans.

The Roman kings of antiquity, and especially Numa, were shown to have impersonated Jupiter:

> In regard to the Roman king, whose priestly functions were inherited by his successor the king of the Sacred Rites, the foregoing discussion has led us to the following conclusions. He represented Jupiter, the great god of the sky, the thunder, and the oak, and in that character made rain, thunder, and lightning for the good of his subjects, like many more kings of the weather in other parts of the world. Further, he not only mimicked the oak god by wearing an oak wreath and other insignia of divinity, but he was married to an oak-nymph Egeria, who appears to have been merely a local form of Diana in her character of goddess of woods, waters, and of childbirth (p. 176).

> Secondly, not only is Numa a personification of Jupiter, but so is the King of the Wood, since Viribus is "a local form of Jupiter" (p. 190). Now the oak was the sacred tree of Jupiter, the supreme god of the Latins. Hence it follows that the King of the Wood, whose life was bound up in a fashion an oak personated no less a deity than Jupiter himself (p. 189).

. . .

> At all events, if I am right in supposing that he passed for a human Jupiter, it would appear that Virbius, with whom legend identified him, was nothing but a local form of Jupiter, considered perhaps in his original aspect as god of the green wood (p. 190).

. . .

The hypothesis that in later times at all events the King of the Wood played the part of the oak god Jupiter, is confirmed by the examination of his divine partner Diana. For two distinct lines of argument converge to show that if Diana was a queen of the woods, in general, she was at Nemi a goddess of the oak in particular. In the first place, she bore the title of Vesta, and as such presided over a perpetual fire, which we have reason to believe was fed with oak wood. But a goddess of fire is not far removed from a goddess of the fuel which burns in the fires; primitive thought drew no fine distinction between the blaze and the wood that blazes. In the second place, the Numph Egeria at Nemi seems to have been merely a form of Diana, and Egeria is definitively said to have been a Dryad, a nymph of the oak (p. 190).

Especially important for the analysis which follows are Frazer's insights into the key role of the god-king in primitive societies as a figure responsible for the cyclical regeneration of both his people and their land, and the way in which Frazer presents the King of the Wood as the prototype of this manner of kingship. Also examined has been the entire set of characters who were in some way bound to the rite at Nemi. These elements will be the most fruitful for the discussion of Benet's utilzation of *The Golden Bough.*

III
Volverás a Región: The Art of
Intertextual Exploitation

The guardian of the forest of Mantua in *Volverás a Región* is called el Numa. Implied in his name is a telescoping of the King of the Wood and the wise king Numa, the two parallel figures who are described by Frazer in *The Golden Bough*. As has already been noted, Benet himself states that this character is modeled on the King of the Wood, and his extra-textual assertion is amply supported by the novel. Moreover, in the article quoted above, he called el Numa "una suerte de vicario en nuestras tierras del guardián del bosque sagrado de Nemi," (p. 160), so that in giving his character the name of the wise Roman king he was eminently conscious of the parallel between Numa and the King of the Wood.

The compression of the two figures into one implies several things. In the first place it is illustrative of the degree to which Benet has assimilated Frazer's argumentation. By telescoping the two figures he demonstrates his awareness of the fact that they are in a sense duplicates of each other, as Frazer suggests. At the same time, by condensing them into one, he sets up an ironic intertextual tension between his character and the presentation of his namesake in Frazer's study. This approach will be considered below when I discuss el Numa's functions.

Not only the name, but the very description of el Numa points directly to Frazer as Benet' source. Outside of the first few pages of his work where he describes the priest at Nemi as grim (p. 1), and stern and sinister (p. 2), the author of *The Golden Bough* provides very little descriptive material concerning the King of the Wood. Benet's description of el Numa is not extensive, though it is somewhat more detailed than that of Frazer's King of the Wood. Nevertheless, the figure who roams the forest at Mantua is described at various junctures of the text of the novel as "astuto y cruel" (p. 11), "fiero" (p. 51), and "extraño" (p. 109), adjectives that are very similar to the ones used by Frazer in his description of the guardian of the grove at Nemi. Other descriptive passages add more details that point to the relationship between the two. For instance, Benet's el Numa is portrayed as armed, although, as befits a modern reelaboration of the King of the Wood, he is "armado de una carabina" (pp. 12-13) instead of a sword with which Frazer's character protected his kingship.[13]

Thus, through his description of el Numa, Benet sets up an intertextual relationship between this figure and the King of the Wood. Another detail of importance is el Numa's advanced age. The first time he is presented in the novel he is not named but is only metonymically described in terms of his function as the "anciano guardián" (p. 8) of the forest at Mantua. At various other moments this insistence on his advanced age is reinforced. Of the eleven passages in the text that in some way refer to his physical description more than half of them emphasize his agedness. He is variously described as the "anciano guardián" (p. 8), "anciana guarda" (p. 110), "viejo" (p. 13; p. 250), "guarda forestal viejo" (p. 181), "viejo guardián de Mantua" (p. 190), and "viejo guarda" (p. 221). Also of interest in terms of the ironic nature of the intertextual relationship is the following description of the character: "... y —al decir del vulgo— de su bandolera cuelga todo

---

13. Most of the other physical details concerning el Numa center on his dress. On several occasions he is described as wearing animal skins. See especially pp. 12 and 250. Several references are also made to his sight. These are, as is the case with many elements in the novel, not in agreement with each other. For example, at one point in the text, the doctor describes el Numa as having "ojos pequeños, negros y vivaces" (p. 250). But only one page earlier, the same character had described the guardian of the grove at Mantua as "torpe, viejo y tuerto" (p. 249).

un rosario formado con las muelas de oro que ha arrancado de sus víctimas" (p. 250). The implicit cannabilistic behavior is significant, but, even more so is the fact that he prowled the forest at Mantua long enough to acquire the artifacts that he removed from the bodies of his victims, a detail that complements the numerous references to his age.

The origin of el Numa as presented in the text of the novel is also interesting since it too contributes to the ironic intertextual web that Benet weaves. While his presence is the regulating factor of life in Región, paradoxically, his very existence is put in doubt several times in the novel. Since no one has ever seen him, there is no absolute certainty of his existence. This nebulousness is supported repeatedly in the work by references to legends that account for his origin and existence, and by references (most of them contradictory) that link his actions to those of important characters and episodes of the *histoire* that are incessantly reiterated in the *discours*. The most extensive account of these is the one provided in Daniel's description.

> Su historia —o su leyenda— es múltiple y contradictoria; se asegura por un lado que se trata de un superviviente carlista que —con más de ciento y pico de años— del odio a las mujeres y a los borbones saca cada año nuevas fuerzas para defender la inviolabilidad del bosque; por el contrario, también cunde la creencia de que su existencia se remonta a muchos años y decenios atrás: un monje hinchado de vanidad que abandona la regla cuando la intransigente reforma moderadora trata de restringir el consuelo del vino... Se afirma también que no se trata sino de un militar que todos hemos conocido y que, habiéndo amado a una mujer hasta la locura, se fugó despechado y se retiró allá para ocultar sus voluntarias mutilaciones y cobrar venganza en el cuerpo de sus seguidores (p. 251).

Daniel's version is founded on popular legends. In it he gives three different explanations of the origin of the guardian of the Mantuan forest, identifying him variously as an aged survivor of the Carlist Wars, a vain monk, and a soldier, whose history is well known to all those in the surrounding area. The soldier so described is of course General Gamallo himself. The incident that the doctor recounts as the one responsible for the general's flight into the forest is the card game. Only in the doctor's version it is Gamallo, as el Numa, who seeks vengeance for his maiming by killing those who had followed him into the mountains in pursuit of the mysterious card player who had run off with María Timoner. This is of interest because on five occasions, three reported by the *extradiégétique* voice and two by the doctor, el Numa is linked to key incidents in the narrative sequence dealing with the card game and what its results augured for the destinies of those involved in it. The repeated allusions to the chase (*cabalgata*) through the mountains in Gamallo's search for vengeance, and of the cloud of dust (*polvareda*) raised by the horseman, have already been discussed in detail. It is interesting to note, however, how Benet ties the chase, which is so essential to the development of both the *histoire* and the *discours*, to the enigmatic figure of el Numa.

Early in the text it is intimated that it is precisely after the chase that el Numa begins to exercise his power over the area.

> Cuando la puerta se cerró —en silencio, sin unir el horror a la fatalidad ni el miedo a la resignación— se había disipado la polvareda: había salido el sol y el abandono de Región se hizo más patente: sopló un aire caliente como el aliento senil de aquel viejo y lanudo Numa, armado de una carabina, que en lo sucesivo guardará el bosque, velando noche y día por toda la extensión de la finca, disparando con infalible puntería cada vez que unos pasos en la hojarasca o los suspiros de un alma cansada, turben la tranquilidad del lugar" (p. 12).

Several pages later the narrator again alludes to the link between the chase through the mountains and el Numa. While describing the vigil undertaken periodically at the church in el Salvador by the few inhabitants of the *comarca* who are left after the war, and who gather there to await the echo of the shot from el Numa's rifle, the narrator injects:

160

Esa misma noche las gentes que lo sintieron pasar acuden con mucha puntualidad a la solitaria torre de la iglesia de El Salvador, para esperar el momento de la confirmación. De noche refresca y en primavera y otoño llega el soplo de la sierra impregnado con el aroma de la luisa y del espliego en el que se mezclan, reviven y vuelven a huir las sombras descompuestas y viciosas de un ayer tantalizado: padres y carruajes y bailes y ríos y libros deshojados, todas las ilusiones y promesas rotas por la polvareda de los jinetes que con la distancia y el tiempo aumentaran de tamaño hasta convertir en grandeza y honor lo que no fue en su día sino ruindad y orgullo, pobreza y miedo (p. 14).

A third instance linking the "legend" of el Numa to the chase occurs a little later in the text: "...todos aquellos combates de caballería que habían de terminar con una intervención milagrosa, anticipación de aquella vengativa cabalgata de viejos señores desbaratada por el guardián del bosque..." (pp. 19-20). The narrator's reference to the fact that it is el Numa who routes Gamallo and his followers in their chase through the mountains in search of vengeance stands in vivid contrast to the "legend" concerning the origin of the guardian of the forest at Mantua as told by Dr. Sebastián. In one of Daniel's three versions, it is Gamallo who becomes el Numa and turns his rage for vengeance on his followers. In the narrator's version, it is el Numa who breaks up the chase, and scatters Gamallo and his followers when they encroach on his domain, thus thwarting the general's attempt to avenge his loss and maiming.

The mountain chase is not the only element of the *histoire* with which the narrator associates el Numa. Toward the end of the novel, the long explanatory footnote hints that el Numa is in fact Luis I. Timoner who fled into the mountains at the war's end and was never seen again.

Pero en cuanto Doctor y en cuanto mentor accidental no podía menos de interrogarse —y de interrogarla— acerca de una conducta que, habiendo dejado tantos puntos oscuros, no sería para

161

justificar una decisión tan grave como su viaje. Aun cuando a veces se trataba de leyenda y otras veces de realidad lo cierto es que existía una finca que en tiempo fue propiedad de Alejandro Cayo Mazón; existía también una fotografía de su pupilo y una requisitoria —que podía comprobarse en cualquier hemeroteca— del Juzgado de Región reclamando la comparecencia de aquellos reos en rebeldía. La sentencia no se hizo pública; solamente el señor Rubal, el único de ellos que fue aprendido, fue sentenciado a la pena capital y desapareció en las sombras de la postguerra al poco tiempo de terminarse la guerra, llevándose consigo los secretos del sumario. Pero en aquella sentencia en rebeldía —y en la fotografía ulteriormente, que no correspondía a la época de la guerra— estaba implícita la supervivencia de unos reos que veinte años después, fueron dados por muertos. Aparte de la leyenda del Numa existían, además los disparos y —como consecuencia confirmatoria— la inviolabilidad del bosque a partir de una revuelta evocadora del camino que el Doctor conocía muy bien a través de una imagen imborrable (p. 275).

By linking the origin and existence of el Numa to a variety of characters and instances essential to the *histoire*, the novelist presents a highly ambiguous character. Nevertheless, the constant repetition of these links in the *discours* provides a parallel with the repetitions of the *histoire* in the *discours* studied in the previous chapter, and serves to highlight the importance of el Numa, making him one of the key recurrent elements of the novel. Also significant is the fact that almost all references to el Numa occur at important junctures in the novel, the *discours* thus being structured in such a way as to lead to the association between principal incidents and characters in the *histoire* and information relevant to this figure. For example information serving to introduce Dr. Sebastián (pp. 9-15) is juxtaposed with allusions to el Numa, his origins and his functions. Another illustration is the fact that on many occasions material delineating details about the guardian is juxtaposed with allusions to the narrative sequence dealing with the card game, and with descriptions pertaining to the Civil War macrounit.

If his origin is cloudy, and his existence somewhat nebulous, the efficacity of el Numa's actions is certain. In effect, the very fact that nobody knows for sure who he is stands in ironic contrast to his role as regulator of life in the area of Región. His origin, then, acts as another element emphasizing the intertextual irony of the figure. Frazer devotes his entire book to proving the beginnings of the rite at Nemi, and the role in it of the King of the Wood, its central figure. The King's counterpart in *Volverás a Región* is equally prominent, but has no such precise beginnings.

While physical description and origin provide an understanding of the nature of the intertextual dialogue that Benet establishes, the pivotal factors mediating the relationship between el Numa and the King of the Wood are to be found in the comparison of their functions. It is in the depiction of functions that all the elements I have examined converge, and that Benet places most of the emphasis in his ironic manipulation of the dialogue between the two works. Like the King of the Wood, el Numa is also a guard and forest sentry. The former wanders incessantly, guarding the grove at Nemi from intruders bent on plucking the Golden Bough and robbing him of both his life and his kinship, while el Numa guards the one at Mantua against the intrusions of strangers who wander there inadvertently. This is mentioned in the first pages of the novel, when the narrator first describes the forest at Mantua.[14]

14. Benet borrows certain descriptive elements directly from Frazer. Early in his study, the English author sets the scene at Nemi as it might have appeared on a Fall night. "Rather we picture to ourselves the scene as it may have been witnessed by a belated wayfarer on one of those wild autumn nights when the dead leaves are falling thick, and the winds seem to sing the dirge of the dying year. It is a sombre picture, set to melancholy music —the background of the forest showing black and jagged against a lowering and stormy sky, the sighing of the wind in the branches, the rustle of the withered leaves under foot, the lapping of the cold water on the shore..." (p. 2). Benet on several occasions in his description of the forest at Mantua refers to the *hojarasca*, and directly ties the description of the dead leaves to el Numa. On one occasion the narrator, while describing el Numa, refers to him as "...disparando con inaliable puntería cada vez que unos pasos en la hojarasca o los suspiros de un alma cansada, turban la tranquilidad del lugar" (p. 12). Later on in the text the doctor also refers to the *hojarasca* in the forest at Mantua, when he mentions el Numa's eyes "que no tienen necesidad de mirar para saber dónde pisa, dónde agita la hoja-

A medida que el camino se ondula y encrespa el paisaje cambia: al monte bajo suceden esas praderas amplias (por donde se dice que pasta una raza salvaje de caballos enanos) de peligroso aspecto erizadas y atravesadas por crestas azuladas y fétidas de caliza carbonífera, semejante al espinazo de un monstruo cuaternario que deja transcurrir su letargo con la cabeza hundida en el pantano; surgen allí, especiadas y delicadas de color, esas flores de montaña de complicada estructura, cochico y miosotis, cantuesos, azaleas de altura y espadaños diminutas hasta que un desprendido e inesperado seto de salgueros y mirtos parece poner fin al viaje con un tronco atravesado a modo de barrera y un anacrónico y casi indescifrable letrero, sujeto a un palo torcido:

Se prohibe el paso
Propiedad privada

Es un lugar tan solitario que nadie —ni en Región, ni en Bocentellas ni en el Puente de Doña Cuativa ni siquiera en la torre de la iglesia de El Salvador— hable de él aún cuando todos saben que raro es el año que el monte no cobra su tributo humano; ese excéntrico extranjero que llega a Región con un coche atestado de bultos y aparatos científicos o el desaventurado e inconsciente cazador que por seguir un rastro o recuperar la gorra arrebatada por el viento va a toparse con esa tumba recién abierta por el anciano guardián, que aun conserva el aroma de la tierra creada y al fondo encharcado de agua (pp. 8-9).

The position of guardian of the grove carries with it for both the King of the Wood and el Numa the necessity that they be assassins or murderers. As Frazer points out "he was a priest and a murderer; and the man for whom he looked was sooner or later to murder him and hold the priesthood in his stead" (p. 1). The same is true of el Numa,

rasca y dónde se estremece el matorral" (p. 250). While it is not strange to find dead and falling leaves in a forest, it is interesting to note this strong similarity between Frazer's and Benet's description.

as the above quotation makes clear. The King of the Wood murders those who enter the Arician grove with the intention of divesting him of his crown. Benet's character murders those who ignore the prohibition written on the weathered sign and attempt to enter the forest at Mantua.

Like his counterpart in the sacred grove of Nemi, however, el Numa is more than just a guardian of a specific area. He is a representative of the aspirations of his people and his land. In him is subsumed their desire for survival. In Frazer's work this desire is seen in the regenerative cycle of death for the sake of rebirth. The King of the Wood is a sympathetic representation of the fertility of his land and the well-being of his subjects. When his powers falter, he must be   replaced, since his weakness is symptomatic of the weakness of his domain. Hence the god must be killed to assure his regeneration.

In *Volverás a Región*, Benet inverts the order. Rather than being responsible for the cyclical regeneration or revival of the area, el Numa is there to maintain the status quo. It is through him that Región is maintained in its state of total ruin, and he is charged with sustaining the futureless present in which the handful of survivors who still reside in the *comarca* live. This is brought out several times in the novel, both by the *extradiégétique* voice and by Dr. Sebastián. At one point the narrator specifically refers to el Numa as the protector of the status quo in Región. "Lo cierto es que nadie se atreve a negar la existencia del hombre al que nadie ha visto pero al que nadie tampoco ha podido llegar a ver y cuya imagen parece presidir y proteger los días de decadencia de esa comarca abandonada y arruinada" (p. 11). Several hundred pages later, the doctor voices a similar opinion about the function of the guardian of Mantua. "Tan es así que sin mucho esfuerzo se llega a pensar hasta qué punto es verosímil esa maldición, hasta qué punto el futuro (¿persistiremos mucho en llamar futuro a eso, el verano de las viudas, las hojas hervidas de la polaca, las reverberaciones urticantes de un pasado dominguero?) ha de seguir determinado por la cerrazón y la puntería y el insomnio de ese viejo guarda" (p. 221). This same idea is reinforced some thirty pages later in the text, in a rather peculiar comment in which the doctor attributes certain ideas to el Numa himself. "¿Por qué esa paz? Sin duda porque no cuentan con el porvenir. El Numa acaba de decir esa misma madrugada 'quedan las cosas como están, el futuro a la mierda'" (p. 253).

In light of the fact that both function as guards, the discinct nature of the "murders" carried out by the two figures becomes even more striking and ironic. The King of the Wood kills to prove he still has the strength that renders him capable of being a regenerative figure. With el Numa, the opposite is true. His "murders" are carried out not to insure regeneration, but rather to maintain the lifelessness of the status quo.

The desire for the maintenance of things as they are is also presented in the text through the numerous references to the periodic vigil that takes place at the tower of the church of El Salvador. The vigil, which has in fact taken on the character of a rite for the few inhabitants who are left in the area, occurs every time strangers approach to break through the residents' hermetically sealed existence. After the strangers pass out of the area on the road that leads through the mountains, the inhabitants gather to wait for the reverberations of el Numa's carbine, proof that their existence has once again been purified.

Esa misma noche las gentes que lo sintieron pasar acuden con puntualidad a la solitaria torre de la iglesia de El Salvador, para esperar el momento de la confirmación. De noche refresca y en primavera y otoño llega el soplo de la sierra impregnado con el aroma de la luisa y del espliego en el que se mezclan, reviven y vuelven a huir las sombras descompuestas y viciosas de un ayer tantalizador: padres y carruajes y bailes y libros deshojados. Todas las ilusiones y promesas rotas por la polvareda de los jinetes que con la distancia y el tiempo aumentarían de tamaño hasta convertir en grandeza y honor lo que no fue en su día sino ruindad y orgullo, pobreza y miedo. No hacen sino escuchar: la torre es tan chica que en el cuerpo de campanas no cabe más de media docena de personas, colgadas sobre el vacío: el resto se ve obligado a esperar en la escalera y —

aun en el corral, en aquellas ocasiones en que ciertos hechos inusitados atraen una mayor concurrencia. No pronuncian una palabra, atentos tan solo a la dirección del viento y el eco que han de traer desde los parajes prohibidos. La espera se acostumbra a ser larga, tan larga como la noche, pero nadie se impacienta: unos minutos antes que las primeras luces del día apunten en el horizonte —ese momento en que los cautivos congregados para emprender un viaje deciden, pasada la primera desazón, desentenderse de sus inquietudes para entregarse al descanso— el sonido del disparo llega envuelto, entre oleadas de menta y verbena, en la incertidumbre de un hecho que, por necesario e indemostrable nunca puede ser evidente. La evidencia llega más tarde, con el alba, la memoria y la esperanza aunadas para repetir el eco de aquel único disparo que debía necesitar el Numa; que sus oidos habían esperado como sentencia de la esfinge al sacrilegio y que, año tras año, aceptaban sin explicaciones ni perplejidad (p. 14).

The same idea is emphasized somewhat further along in the text. In this instance the journey to El Salvador, and the waiting for the confirmation of el Numa's unerring marksmanship are actually referred to by the narrator as a type of rite.

Ciertamente todo el país padecía una enfermedad crónica y una epidemia porque (aparte de que nadie podía sentirse atraído por el misterio del agua) en la conciencia popular se había llegado a considerar punible, insensata e imprudente la más ligera advertencia acerca de los atractivos del monte: era ese punto de hipocresía lo que concedía al viaje anual el valor de un rito, el misterio de una fe y el sentido de una confirmación (p. 145).

The reference to the word rite in the context of the novel's relationship with *The Golden Bough* amplifies the irony of the reversal of functions that Benet undertakes. There is an ironic contrast between the rite celebrated at El Salvador by the surviving residents of the *comarca*, or the rite that they await there, and the one in the Arician grove.[15] Again, the latter has as its goal the regeneration of the people, while the former has as its end the maintenance of the status quo. In this light it is interesting that Benet has not chosen to give to el Numa a parallel version of the female consort enjoyed by the Kings of the Wood. The nature of the relationship between the two works makes this particular omission significant.[16] By not having a female consort for el Numa, Benet highlights the nonregenerative nature of el Numa's office. The exclusion of a parallel figure in Benet's novel argues strongly that in *Volverás a Región* the idea of regeneration has been replaced by that of the steritily inherent in keeping things as they are and resisting all intrusions into the hermetically sealed, futureless existence of the *comarca*.

Of interest in the same light is the double irony contained in the very name of the place where the vigil is carried out: El Salvador. In terms of its meaning in the context of the narrative discourse, it is of no little significance that the spot at which the surviving inhabitants gather to await confirmation that the status quo has been restored should be called El Salvador. This vividly underlines the idea that for those who live in the area, salvation is equated with purification of the hermetic existence they so fervently desire. But the place name is also significant in terms of the ironic intertextual dialogue carried out with *The Golden Bough*. The rite at Nemi, as I have had occasion to state many times in the course of this chapter, has as its ultimate aim the assurance of the regeneration of the area and the people. In this sense its goal is their "salvation," although in a telluric and not a theological sense, through the continued fecundity of people, animals and land. The parallel rite in *Volverás a Región* is passively awaited by the survi-

---

15. I refer to the ritual of the survivors as passive because it consists of nothing more than awaiting the more important ritual of el Numa's periodic action.

16. One of the most significant omissions is that of the oak tree and the Golden Bough that grew from it. It is, of course, a central element in the rite at the Arician grove, since the person wishing to succeed to the position of King of the Wood had first to pluck the Golden Bough from the tree. While the oak is not a central element in the rite at Mantua, it nevertheless does appear in the text, and does play an important role in the relationship between the two works under discussion here.

168

vors of the *comarca* at a spot called El Salvador, but the salvation they desire stands in ironic contrast to fecundity and regeneration.

At the same time, the nature of the rite performed in *Volverás a Región* is indicative of the passive nature of the survivors' relationship to both the rite and to el Numa. As in the quotation adduced from page fourteen of the novel ascertains, the survivors accept el Numa's action without explanation. Their passivity is also brought out in the following passage.

En Región apenas se habla de Mantua ni de su extraño guardián: no se habla de él en ninguno de los pueblos de la vega, ni en Región ni en Bocentellas ni en el Puente de Doña Cautiva ni siquiera en la torre de la iglesia abandonada de El Salvador esas pocas noches — tres o cuatro cada década— en que unos cuantos supervivientes de la comarca (menos de treinta vecinos que no se hablan ni se saludan y que a duras penas se recuerdan, reunidos por un instinto común de supervivencia, exagerado por la soledad, o por un viejo ritual cuyo significado se ha perdido y en él que se representan los misterios de su predestinación) se congregan allí para escuchar el eco de unos disparos que, no se afirma pero se cree, proceden de Mantua. Lo cierto es que nadie se atreve a negar la existencia del hombre al que nadie ha visto pero al que nadie tampoco ha podido llegar a ver y cuya imagen parece presidir y proteger los días de decadencia de esa comarca abandonada y arruinada: un anciano guarda, astuto y cruel, cubierto de lanas crudas como un pastor tártaro y calzado con abarcas de cuerda, dotado del don de ubicuidad dentro de los límites de la propiedad que recorre día y noche con los ojos cerrados (p. 11).

The ritual persists, since the ability of el Numa to perpetuate the inviolable ruin of the *comarca* remains effective. Its origin, however, has been forgotten, and, what is more it has gone amok.

El Numa, unlike the figure on whom he is modeled, is not inhibited by any restrictions or taboos. The final taboo placed on the King of the Wood, and on all ancient priest-kings was their death, which took place when their power failed, or when they became aged. This is of course not true of el Numa, who has grown old and has never been replaced. It is in this context that the numerous references to el Numa's advanced age become meaningful. They represent still another ironic use of the intertextual dialogue between the King of the Wood and Benet's character. Frazer describes the heaviness with which the crown weighed on the head of the King of the Wood. "The least relaxation of his vigilance, the smallest abatement of his strength of limb or still of fence, put him in jeopardy, grey hairs might seal his death warrant" (p. 2). But Benet has the narrator of *Volverás a Región* repeatedly point to the longevity of el Numa's tenure in his position, and his advanced age. El Numa, it appears, is not subject to removal.

In addition, there are other references to the unchecked nature of his control over the survivors of the *comarca*, who, as we have seen, are but passive spectators to the rite that regulates their existence. One such example can be found when the narrator refers to the "cruel e insaciable apetito de revancha del viejo guardián de Mantua" (p. 190). The ironic distance established in this case between the functions of the King of the Wood and el Numa is patent. The latter, unrestrained by any controls, not only maintains the status quo in the area, but acts in a way almost diametrically opposed to the comportment of his counterpart.

The ironic use of intertextuality that Benet employs is thus solidified through the examination of the functions with which he endows his character. In the first place, he establishes a tension between the funcions of the wise king Numa, who as legend had it, was responsible for giving laws to the Roman tribes, and the guardian of the forest of Mantua, who bears the former's name, but none of his characteristics. This ironic distancing is further intensified by the manner in which the Spanish novelist structures the relationship between el Numa and the King of the Wood. The symbol of the need for regeneration in *The Golden Bough* becomes in Benet's novel the symbol of Región's desire for things to remain as they are. That desire is repeatedly characterized by a state of ruin, and a futureless present which, through the eventual attrition of the surviving inhabitants, will lead ultimately to nonexistence. Thus the regenerative cycle inherent in the figure of the King of the Wood, and in his office, is broken, and a straight line results, one headed inevitably for the polar opposite of regeneration: complete and total destruction.

In this manner the intertextual exploitation of el Numa and his model the King of the Wood reinforces the idea of final ruin presented in the structure of the novel's *histoire* and *discours*. Juan Benet has shrewdly utilized the intertextual dialogue he opens with one of the classics of twentieth-century thought, in order to intensify the ideology underlying the structure of *Volverás a Región*. But the importance of the ironic intertextual dialogue does not end with the relationship between el Numa and the King of the Wood. Benet also exploits it in his articulation of the narrative space in which the novel transpires.

Many of the critics who have dealt with this novel have discussed the vital role that Región's imposing physical geography plays in its development. It has also often been pointed out that the narrative space in which the work develops is imbued with strange and inexplicable elements that contrast with the precise nature with which Benet fixes the area's physical location and description. These elements have been used to support postulations of Benet's desire to provide the work's setting with a mythic atmosphere.[17] While there is no doubt that the narrative space created by the author plays a fundamental part in the novel, I cannot concur with those critics who see mythic overtones in it. An attempt to explain away all the mysterious or enigmatic factors in *Volverás a Región* is impossible, precisely because on occasions Benet leaves certain aspects unresolved. One may, on the other hand, focus more efficiently on certain of them in the light of the ironic intertextual dialogue carried on with Sir James Frazer's work. The rea-

17. Among the most important is Ricardo Gullón's *Insula* study cited on a number of occasions. See also pp. 44-49 of Herzberger's monograph. Andrei Ionescu's "Explorarea unui spatiu mitic," *Seculol XX*, Nos. 166-167 (1974), pp. 87-92 and Michael Thomas' unpublished dissertation "Myth and Archetype in the New Spanish Novel (1950-1970): a Study in Changing Novelistic Techniques," University of Kansas, 1976.

der who is aware of the existence, and the nature of this dialogue will perceive these seemingly mythic or mysterious elements in a different manner.[18]

In the preceding pages I have attempted in essence to "demythify" both the place, and its mysterious inhabitant, and to point out how these supposedly mythic elements are in fact the result of Benet's shrewd use of intertextuality. Other aspects of the setting such as the stunted oaks that are a part of Región's physical geography can also be better understood in this manner. Apparently a somewhat enigmatic and highly innocuous factor in the overall structure of the work, the oaks take on a great degree of meaning for the reader with the literary competence necessary to construe them as an element of the dialogue with *The Golden Bough*. Several references to these oaks are found early in the novel, when the narrator details the physical setting of the area.

> ...se extiende ante el viajero toda la inmensa desolación del páramo: una llanada estéril (a la que por los rigores del clima le niegan incluso la vegetación de los desiertos y donde sólo aciertan a arraigar algunas plantas de constitución primitiva, crucíferas y esquisetos, helechos y cardos que han perdurado desde las edades paleozóicas gracias, en parte, a su infecundidad) orlada en su horizonte por un festón cambiante, casi imaginario de robles enanos (pp. 40-41).

Several pages later, the narrator again mentions these dwarf oaks. "Porque en verano allí solo vuelan los insectos: ese monte bajo cubierto de brezo, carquesas y roble enano que no da sombra..." (p. 47). In my opinion it is far from fortuitous that Benet should characterize the oak trees in Región as stunted. The oak, as was demonstrated in the second section of this chapter, is a pivotal element in the expla-

---

18. The same holds true if one is aware of the intertextual link between Euclides da Cunha's *Os Sertões*, a socio-historical chronicle of the Canudos expedition, and *Volverás a Región*. This relationship is analyzed in my essay "Región's Brazilian Backlands."

nation of the rite at Nemi. The tree from which the candidate for the title of King of the Wood had to pluck the Golden Bough is identified by Frazer as an oak. In addition, the King of the Wood was viewed as a type of oak deity, and in this way was linked to Jupiter, the supreme god of the Romans, himself an oak deity. Hence, given the implications of the oak in Frazer's work, Benet's description of the oaks in the *comarca* of Región as dwarfs is no accident. It serves ironically to distance the stunted variety found in *Volverás a Región* from their counterpart in *The Golden Bough*, where it is associated with the destinies of gods. Once again there is an instance where purportedly mythic elements are in fact skillfully contrived aspects of the dialogue with Frazer's study.

A similar intertextual explanation can be found for the mysterious red flowers that grow in Región, and which make up another strange component of the work's setting. Herzberger explains these flowers in terms of the concept of magical realism so often used in critical appraisals of modern Latin American literature.[19] However, a knowledge of the source of this strange flower leads to a fuller appreciation of its presence and function in *Volverás a Región*.

This seemingly mysterious aspect of Región's enigmatic flora is described by Dr. Sebastián, as part of his description to Gamallo's daughter of certain features of the area's geography.

Son los cálices, al decir de los pastores, que guardan la sangre del padre Abraham, y del rey Sidonio y del valeroso Aviza —el joven protestón— y de todos los caballeros cristianos que a lo largo de los siglos han caído en los combates del Torce y de los que se alimentaba en su niñez aquel Drácula rural de comienzos del siglo —el vampiro Atilano— que en los primeros días de junio —cuando las flores marchitan y se abren sus secas bayas para extender por doquier unas bolas pequeñas, rugosas y pardas como alcaparras—,

19. "One of the most striking elements involved in the use of magical realism is the red flower which grows wild in the mountains of Región" (Herzberger, *Novelistic World*, p. 48).

bajaba de noche hasta las tapias de Bocentellas, de El Salvador, Etán y Región, envuelto hasta la cabeza con una manta de paja, la boca coloreada de un tinte vegetal; también es la sangre de todos los que cayeron en aquellos pagos, víctimas de su impaciencia y del cruel e insaciable apetito de revancha del viejo guardián de Mantua. Es la flor de la inquietud, de la desazón del alma, de los contrastes del espíritu, de su impulsivo anhelo que se apodera de la voluntad para conquistar las alturas cuando los primeros días temerados despejan las nubes que las han ocultado durante todo el invierno, para envolverlas con un halo morado, preludio de la sequía... El paisano la maldice, no la coge jamás ni la extirpa ni se atreve a llevar el ganado allá donde ella brota. El día que distraído la pisa, da un salto atrás, cae de hinojos y se persigna tantas veces cuantas flores se hallan a su vista; y si ha llegado a aplastarla o romperla la costumbre le obliga a practicarse un pequeño corte en el dedo y, a fin de redimir su falta y aplacar el enojo del muerto hollado, vierte unas gotas de su propia sangre sobre el tallo cortado. Porque nace siempre donde descansa un resto humano, un hueso o un escapulario que está pidiendo venganza, recuerdo y redención al mundo de los vivos. Tan considerable es la fuerza de la maldición que en más de una ocasión el paisano que ha visto sus sembrados tapizados por el repentino brote solferino (un pelillo temblón y urticante) no lo ha pensado dos veces: sin lágrimas, desesperación ni aspavientos ha recogido el ganado y la familia, ha llamado a sus vecinos para decir adiós, ha subido sus trastos al carro y —según la magnitud de sus culpas o sus remordimientos— ha cerrado la casa y los corrales y se ha marchado de allí, tras prenderles fuego. Y puede también que sea la flor de Mitra, de que habla algún geógrafo romano, y que más tarde buscarán en sus peregrinaciones, en el fondo de los precipicios y en las venerables grutas de los santos, aquellos grandes pecadores de la alta edad media para quienes ni Roma ni la ascesis sabían encontrar la penitencia adecuada (pp. 189-191).

This unusual flower, its origins, and the strange control it has over the inhabitants of the area is related to the section of Frazer's study dealing with a similar type of flower. While this part of *The Golden Bough* does not bear directly on the rite at Nemi, it is important to it, since it deals with the death and resurrection of gods in other cultures.

> The Phoenician festival appears to have been a vernal one, for its date was determined by the discoloration of the river Adonis, and this has been observed by modern travelers to occur in spring. At that season the red earth washed down from the mountains by the rain tinged the water of the river, and even the sea, for a great way with a blood-red hue, and the crimson stain was believed to be the blood of Adonis, actually wounded to death by the boar on Mount Lebanon. Again, the scarlet anemone is said to have sprung from the blood of Adonis, or to have been stained by it; and as the anemone blooms in Syria about Easter, this may be though to show that the festival of Adonis, or at least one of his festivals, was held in the spring. The name of the flower is probably derived from Naaman ("darling"), which seems to have been an epithet of Adonis. The Arabs still call the anemone "wounds of Naaman." The red rose also was said to owe its hue to the same sad occasion; for Aphrodite, hastening to her wounded love, trod on a bush of white roses; the cruel thorns tore her tender flesh, and her sacred blood dyed the white roses forever red. It would be idle, perhaps, to lay much weight on evidence drawn from the calendar of flowers, and in particular to press an argument so fragile as the bloom of the rose. Yet so far as it counts at all, the tale which links the damask rose to the death of Adonis points to a summer rather than to a spring celebration of his passion (pp. 390-391).

In this instance too, the use of the intertextual source creates an ironic distance between the description in Benet's novel and that offered by Frazer. In the one case we have a flower colored by the death of a god, which is used by Frazer in his discussion of the cyclical regeneration of gods in general. In *Volverás a Región*, the flower is not linked to regeneration, but once again to the atmosphere of sterility and destruction that permeates the entire work.

To reiterate, I do not mean to suggest that the perception of the intextextual link between *Volverás a Región* and *The Golden Bough* eradicates all the enigmatic and at times contradictory aspects of Benet's novel. It does, nevertheless, belie the attribution of this atmosphere of mystery to Benet's desire to create a mythic narrative ambience, since this type of interpretation overlooks the significance of both the presence and nature of the dialogue.

The narrative space of the novel can, then, only be construed as mythic or wholly mysterious if this dialogue is ignored. Once it is perceived, much of the mystery vanishes, and the reader comes to understand the ironic tension that Benet manipulates. Región is less mysterious if it is seen as the polar opposite of its model. In this light, its formidable and inhospitable narrative space becomes even more important in the work. The ambience in which the novel transpires serves not only to mediate the progress of the action and characters articulated in the *histoire*, but also to underscore the structural message inherent in both it and the *discours*. This ironic dialogue distances the setting of *Volverás a Región* from the sylvan landscape of Nemi, described by Frazer in the first pages of *The Golden Bough*. At the same time, it reflects the change wrought by the Spanish novelist in the concept of cyclical regeneration so essential in Frazer's study. Seen from this perspective, the repeated reference to the imposing and destructive nature of the environs of Región support this fundamental change. Once cognizant of this, the reader can evaluate the description of the setting in terms of the way Benet distances it from that in the work with which his novel enters into intertextual dialogue. The knowing reader is thus able to see that rather than being wholly mysterious and mythic, the narrative space is a functional element in the intertextual relationship, and, as such, underscores the idea that Región's ruin is fundamentally attributable to the effects of the Civil War, a concept that illuminates the ideological message inherent in the structure of the novel's *histoire* and *discours*.

CONCLUSION

Spain and its cultural production have undergone enormous changes since the Insurgent forces' victory in the Civil War installed the francoist regime in power in 1939. Yet the nature of the dialectical relationship between culture and mediating ambience has often been lost in studies analyzing the arts of this era because of the utilization of methodologies unable to measure the way culture and society are linked. In addition, the fundamental misconception that the passage of time and a marked improvement in quality attenuated the ideological bases of fiction dealing with the Civil War contributes to the confusion. This monograph, to the contrary, insists upon the underlying non-changeable elements of francoist ideology and their effect on culture under Franco. The tension resulting from this ideological domination cleaves the cultural sector into two antithetical groupings, one supportive of the regime, one critical of it. These two world views inform both the content and structural disposition of Spain's literature even into the period when the newer complex organization of these evolving modes seemingly shows no direct ideological bias vis-à-vis the war and/or Franco's Spain.

The incorporation of a new critical model rooted in the dialectical literary sociology of Lucien Goldmann has enabled me to avoid what I see as the shortcomings of previous evaluations. Goldmann's perception that world view is articulated at the level of aesthetic organization and not exclusively at that of content displaces emphasis from the reflection of ideas in the surface manifestation of the text to the recognition of the existence of a homological relationship between narrative *dispositio* and the structure of the world view of the author's collective subject.

179

Fusing Goldmann's theoretical postulations with elements of structuralist narratology permits a more efficient analysis of the aesthetic organization of narrative discourse, especially its syntactical disposition. This study of narrative syntax is based on the assumption that the syntagmatic order of both the *histoire* and *discours* manifest a homological relationship to the author's world view. Paradigmatic aspects such as intertextuality and the creation of narrative space also contribute to this appraisal.

Juan Benet's *Volverás a Región* represents a watershed in modern peninsular literature, and critics have consistently placed it at the forefront of those narrative texts responsible for changing the direction followed by Spanish fiction and for rearticulating the parameters of fictive discourse treating the Spanish Civil War. It is paradoxically fitting that a critical model rooted in concepts that link literature to the specificity of its own socio-political environment be tested on a text which apparently demonstrates no such connection. The introduction to Benet offered in Chapter II lays the foundation for the analysis of *Volverás a Región*, disavowing prior treatments of the novelist and demonstrating that a careful reading of his essayistic production allows one to locate him within the space of the anti-regime collective subject discussed in Chapter I.

Based on this information one can proceed to the specific text under consideration, whose structure homologically echoes that of the anti-regime collective subject. Its *histoire* charts a one-directional path toward decadence and decay predicated on the effects the Civil War held out for those in some way touched by it. This is carried out in the text through the manner in which the action's two key events (the card game and war) affect all the actors who have a significant role in the narrative.

In a similar way the structure of the *discours* is also meaning-bearing. The disposition of the sequences of the *histoire* in the *discours* demonstrates a syntactical organization whose underlying message parallels that of the *histoire* through the manner in which it orients the reader's perceptions of key moments in the text's action. Other temporal aspects emphasize this ordering process, as do *mode* and *voix* which control the way the text is presented to the reader.

The ideological message demonstrable at the syntagmatic level is also perceptible at the paradigmatic one. Benet's portrayal of narrative space and the intertextual link between his novel and *The Golden Bough* bear this out. The ironic inversion of meaning which characterizes the latter relationship change the regenerative King of the Wood into the non-regenerative figure of el Numa so as to reinforce the world view articulated in the book's narrative syntax.

The analytical framework brought to the study of Benet's first novel is applicable to all fiction produced in Spain during the francoist period regardless of whether it treats the Civil War. Narrative discourse's passage through the most far-removed recesses of neo-baroque complexity need no longer lead analysts to herald or denounce (depending on one's proclivities) peninsular fiction's breaking of its link with the repressive environment in which it was produced. By establishing a methodology which joins meaning to structure and not merely to content, and by articulating an apparatus capable of unraveling even the most complex of narratives, it is hoped that this study provides a new critical context in whose space a substantial reevaluation of Spanish fiction can be undertaken.

The writing of this book was motivated by the attempt to seek a solution to the complex relationship of textual immanence and societal mediation, an issue that has occupied its author for a number of years. In the academy there is always the desire to produce *the* definitive work of scholarship on a given topic. Yet training in dialectics forces one to realize both the impossibility and inappropriateness of a quest of that sort. If the issues addressed in the preceding pages stir a critical dialogue through whose dialectical movement we come to better understand not only the nature of the original question of method here addressed, but the boundaries of literary creation in Franco's Spain as well, this book shall have fulfilled the intent that inspired it.

BIBLIOGRAPHY

The bibliography for this volume is limited to first footnote citations and other important sources mentioned in the body of the text. More complete information on Benet is available in Malcolm Compitello's "Juan Benet and His Critics," *Anales de la Novela de Postguerra*, 3(1978), 123-141. A greatly expanded and up-dated version of this essay will appear in a volume of essays on Benet, *Approaches to Juan Benet,* ed. Roberto Manteiga, David Herzberger, and Malcolm Compitello, now in press at the University Press of New England. Studies on Civil War Fiction are analyzed in my "The Novel, The Critics and The Civil War: A Bibliographic Essay," *Anales de la Narrativa Española Contemporánea*, 4(1979), 117-138. An extensive listing of studies on Franco's Spain, and modern poetics are found in my dissertation "Ordering the Evidence: The Vision of the Spanish Civil War in Post-War Spanish Fiction," Indiana University, Bloomington, 1979.

Aveleyra, Teresa. "Algo sobre las criaturas de Juan Benet." *Nueva Revista de Filología Hispánica*, 23 (1974), 121-130.

Bakhtin, Mikhail. *Problems in Dostoevsky's Poetics*, trans. William Rotsel. Ann Arbor, Michigan: Ardis, 1973.

Benet, Juan. Answers to *encuesta* on literature and education in Spain. In *Literature y educación*, ed. Fernando Lázaro Carreter. Madrid: Castalia, 1974, pp. 197-206.

———. "Barojiana." In Benet, Juan *et al, Barojiana*. Madrid: Taurus, 1972, pp. 11-45.

———. "Breve historia de *Volverás a Región.*" *Revista de Occidente*, NS 134 (May 1976), pp. 160-165.

———. "Una época troyana." In *En ciernes*. Madrid: Taurus, 1976, pp. 85-102.

———. "Historia editorial y judicial de *Volverás a Región.*" In *La moviola de Eurípides*. Madrid: Taurus, 1981, pp. 31-44.

———. "*La inspiración y el estilo*, 2nd ed. Barcelona: Seix Barral, 1974.

———. "Una leyenda: Numa." In *Del pozo y del Numa: Un ensayo y una leyenda*. Barcelona: La Gaya Ciencia, 1978, pp. 96-168.

———. *¿Qué fue la guerra civil?* Barcelona: La Gaya Ciencia, 1976.

———. "Reflexiones sobre Galdós." *Cuadernos para el Diálogo*, Número Extra 23 (December 1970), pp. 13-15.

———. Remarks made at Ciclo de Novela Española Contemporánea, Fundación Juan March, 2-7 June 1975. Rpt. *Novela española actual*, ed. Andrés Amorós. Madrid: Fundación Juan March/ Editorial Castalia, 1977, pp. 173-178.

———. Remarks made during participation in the "Mesa redonda sobre novela." *Cuadernos para el Diálogo*, Número Extra 23 (December 1970), pp. 45-52.

———. "Respuesta al Sr. Montero" *Cuadernos para el Diálogo*, Número Extra 23 (December 1970) pp. 75-76.

———. *Volverás a Región*. Barcelona: Destino, 1967.

Cabrera, Vicente. *"Volverás a Región"*: An Antithetical Pattern of Enigma." Unpublished manuscript.

Campbell, Federico. *Infame turba*. Barcelona: Lumen, 1971.

Compitello, Malcolm Alan. "The Cultural Ideologies of Franco's Spain." Unpublished manuscript.

———. "Juan Benet and His Critics". *Anales de la Novela de Postguerra*, 3 (1978), 123-141.

————. "The Novel, The Critics, and the Spanish Civil War: A Bibliographic Essay." *Anales de la Narrativa Española Contemporánea*, 4 (1979), 117-138.

————. "Ordering the Evidence: The Vision of the Spanish Civil War in Post-War Spanish Fiction." Unpublished Dissertation, Indiana University, Bloomington, 1979.

————. "The Paradoxes of Praxis: Juan Benet and Modern Poetics." In *Approaches to Juan Benet*, ed. Roberto Manteiga, David Herzberger and Malcolm Compitello. Hanover, New Hampshire: University Press of New England, in press.

————. "Región's Brazilian Backlands: The Link Between *Volverás a Región* and Euclides da Cunha's *Os Sertões*." *Hispanic Journal*, 1, No. 2 (Spring 1980), 25-45.

————. *Volverás a Región*", the Critics and the Spanish Civil War". *The American Hispanist*, 4 No. 36 (May 1979), 11-20.

Corrales Egea, José. *La novela española actual: Ensayo de ordenación*. Madrid: Cuadernos para el Diálogo, 1971.

Costa, Luis. "El lector-viajero en *Volverás a Región*." *Anales de la Narrativa Española Contemporánea*, 4 (1979), 9-19.

Ferreras, Juan Ignacio. *Fundamentos de sociología literaria*. Madrid: Cátedra, 1980.

————. "Le problème du sujet collectif en littérature." *Actes, Picaresque Espagnol. Etudes Sociocritiques*. Monpellier: CERS, 1976, pp. 57-67.

————. "La sociología de Lucien Goldmann." *Revista de Occidente*, NS 105 (December 1971), pp. 311-336.

Frazer, Sir James. *The Golden Bough*. New York: MacMillian, 1963.

————. *The Golden Bough*, ed. Theodor H. Gaster. New York: Mentor Books, 1964.

García Rico, Eduardo. *Literatura y política. En torno al realismo español*. Madrid: Cuadernos para el Diálogo, 1971.

Genette, Gérard. "Discours du récit." In *Figures III*. Paris: Seuil, 1972, pp. 67-282.

———. *Narrative Discourse. An Essay in Method*, trans. Jane E. Lewin. Ithaca: Cornell University Press, 1980.

Gimferrer, Pere "El pensamiento literario (1939-1976)." In *La cultura bajo el franquismo*, ed. José María Castellet. Barcelona: Ediciones de Bolsillo, 1977, pp. 105-130.

———. "Sobre Juan Benet." *Plural: Revista Mensual de Excelsior*, No. 17 (February 1973), pp. 13-16.

Goldmann, Lucien. "The Genetic-Structuralist Method in the History of Literature." In *Towards a Sociology of the Novel*, trans., Alan Sheridan. Cambridge: Tavistock Publications, 1975, pp. 156-181.

———. *The Hidden God*, trans., Phillip Thody. London: Routledge and Kegan Paul, 1970.

———. "Littérature (Sociologie de la)." Enciclopaedia Universalis. Paris: Enciclopaedia Universalis France, S.A., 1968.

———. *Marxisme et Sciences Humaines*. Paris: Gallimard, 1970.

Grant, Michael and John Hazel. *Gods and Mortals in Classical Mythology*. Springfield, Massachussets: G & S Merriam, 1976.

Guerin, Wilfred L. *et al. A Handbook of Critical Approaches to Literature*. New York: Harper and Row, 1966.

Gullón, Ricardo. "Una región laberíntica que bien pudiera llamarse España." *Insula*, No. 319 (June 1973), pp. 3, 10.

Hendricks, William O. "Methodology of Narrative Structural Analysis." *Essays on Semio-Linguistics and Verbal Art*. The Hague: Mouton, 1973, pp. 175-195.

Herzberger, David K. "Enigma as Narrative Determinant in Juan Benet." *Hispanic Review*, 49 (1979), 149-157.

———. *The Novelistic World of Juan Benet*. Clear Creek, Indiana: The American Hispanist, 1977.

————. "Theoretical Approaches to the Spanish New Novel: Juan Benet and Juan Goytisolo". *Revista de Estudios Hispánicos*, 14, No. 2 (May 1980), 3-17.

Martínez Torrón, Diego. "Juan Benet o los márgenes de la sorpresa." In Benet, Juan, *Un viaje de invierno*, ed. Diego Martínez Torrón. Madrid: Cátedra, 1980, pp. 11-110.

Mignolo, Walter. "La noción de competencia en poética." *Cuadernos Hispanoamericanos*, No. 300 (June 1975), pp. 605-622.

Monleón, José. *Treinta años de teatro de derecha*. Barcelona: Tusquets, 1971.

Montero, Isaac. "Acotaciones a una mesa redonda: respuestas a Juan Benet y defensa apresurada del realismo." *Cuadernos para el Diálogo*, Número Extra 23 (December 1970), pp. 65-74.

————. "La novela española de 1955 hasta hoy: una crisis de dos exaltaciones antagónicas." *Triunfo*, Número Extra 507 17 June 1972, pp. 86-94.

Nelson, Esther. "The Aesthetics of Refraction: A Comparative Study of *Pedro Páramo* and *Volverás a Región*." Unpublished manuscript.

————. "Narrative Perspective in *Volverás a Región*." *The American Hispanist*, 4 No. 36 (May 1979), 3-6.

Núñez, Antonio. "Encuentro con Juan Benet." *Insula*, No. 269 (April 1969), p. 4.

Oliart, Alberto. "Viaje a Región." *Revista de Occidente*, NS 80 (November 1969), pp. 224-234.

Oltra, Benjamín. *Pensar en Madrid*. Barcelona: Euros, 1976.

Ortega, José: "Estudios sobre la obra de Juan Benet." *Cuadernos Hispanoamericanos*, No. 284 (February 1974), pp. 229-258.

Pérez Firmat, Gustavo. "Apuntes para un modelo de intertextualidad en literatura." *Romanic Review*, 79 (1978), 1-19.

189

Perojo, Benito. "Hacia la creación de una cinematografía nacional." *Vértice: Revista Nacional de la Falange*, No. 1 (April 1937), n. p.

The Princeton Encyclopedia of Poetry and Poetics, ed. Alex Preminger *et al.* Princeton, New Jersey: Princeton University Press, 1966.

Rodríguez Padrón, Jorge. "Apuntes para una teoría benetiana." *Insula*, Nos. 396-397 (November-December 1979), pp. 3,5.

Rutherford, John. "Story, Character, Setting and Narrative in Galdos' *El amigo Manso.*" In *Style and Structure in Literature. Essays in the New Stylistics*, ed. Roger Fowler. Ithaca, New York: Cornell University Press, 1975, pp. 177-212.

Sastre, Alfonso. "Poco más que anécdotas 'culturales' alrededor de quince años (1950-1966)." *Triunfo*, Número Extra. No. 507 17 June 1972, pp. 81-85.

Scholes, Robert. *Structuralism in Literature. An Introduction.* New Haven: Yale University Press, 1974.

Solomon, Barbara Probst. *Arriving Where We Started.* New York: Harper and Row, 1972.

Spires, Robert. *"Volverás a Región* y la desintegración total." In *La novela española de postguerra.* Barcelona: CUPSA, 1978, pp. 224-246.

Summerhill, Stephen. "Prohibition and Transgression in Two Novels of Juan Benet." *The American Hispanist*, 4, No. 36 (May 1979), 20-24.

Todorov, Tzvetan. *Grammaire du Décameron.* The Hague: Mouton, 1969.

Tola de Habich, Fernando and Patricia Grieve. *Los españoles y el boom.* Caracas: Editorial Tiempo Nuevo, 1971.

Vázquez Montalbán, Manuel. "La pervertida sentimentalidad de Pío Baroja." In *Barojiana.* Madrid: Taurus, 1972, pp. 155-176.

Vickery, John B. *The Literary Impact of The Golden Bough.* Princeton, New Jersey: Princeton University Press, 1973.

Villanueva, Darío. "La novela de Juan Benet." *Camp de L'Arpa,* No. 8 (November 1973), pp. 9-16.

Wescott, Julia Lupinacci. "Exposition and Plot in Benet's *Volverás a Región.*" *Kentucky Romance Quarterly*, 28 (1981), 155-163.